3200764 941

House of Commons
Committee of Public Accounts

Foot and Mouth Disease: applying the lessons

Ninth Report of Session 2005–06

Report, together with formal minutes, oral and written evidence

Ordered by The House of Commons to be printed 17 October 2005

HC 563
Incorporating HC 387-i, Session 2004–05
Published on 1 November 2005
by authority of the House of Commons
London: The Stationery Office Limited
£11.00

The Committee of Public Accounts

The Committee of Public Accounts is appointed by the House of Commons to examine "the accounts showing the appropriation of the sums granted by Parliament to meet the public expenditure, and of such other accounts laid before Parliament as the committee may think fit" (Standing Order No 148).

Current membership

Mr Edward Leigh MP (*Conservative, Gainsborough*) (Chairman)
Mr Richard Bacon MP (*Conservative, South Norfolk*)
Angela Browning MP (*Conservative, Tiverton and Honiton*)
Mr Alistair Carmichael MP (*Liberal Democrat, Orkney and Shetland*)
Mr Greg Clark MP (*Conservative, Tunbridge Wells*)
Rt Hon David Curry MP (*Conservative, Skipton and Ripon*)
Mr Ian Davidson MP (*Labour, Glasgow South West*)
Helen Goodman MP (*Labour, Bishop Auckland*)
Mr John Healey MP (*Labour, Wentworth*)
Diana R Johnson MP (*Labour, Hull North*)
Mr Sadiq Khan MP (*Labour, Tooting*)
Sarah McCarthy-Fry MP (*Labour, Portsmouth North*)
Jon Trickett MP (*Labour, Hemsworth*)
Kitty Ussher MP (*Labour, Burnley*)
Rt Hon Alan Williams MP (*Labour, Swansea West*)
Mr Stephen Williams MP (*Liberal Democrat, Bristol West*)

Powers

Powers of the Committee of Public Accounts are set out in House of Commons Standing Orders, principally in SO No 148. These are available on the Internet via www.parliament.uk.

Publications

The Reports and evidence of the Committee are published by The Stationery Office by Order of the House. All publications of the Committee (including press notices) are on the Internet at http://www.parliament.uk/pac. A list of Reports of the Committee in the present Session is at the back of this volume.

Committee staff

The current staff of the Committee is Nick Wright (Clerk), Christine Randall (Committee Assistant), Emma Sawyer (Committee Assistant), Ronnie Jefferson (Secretary), and Luke Robinson (Media Officer).

Contacts

All correspondence should be addressed to the Clerk, Committee of Public Accounts, House of Commons, 7 Millbank, London SW1P 3JA. The telephone number for general enquiries is 020 7219 5708; the Committee's email address is pubaccom@parliament.uk.

Contents

Report

Page

Summary 3
    Implementation of previous recommendations 3
    Further action is required, however, in two key areas: 3

Conclusions and recommendations 5

1   Controlling and sharing the costs of a further epidemic 7

2   Preparations for a future epidemic 9

3   Vaccination or cull 11

Formal minutes 14

Witnesses 15

List of written evidence 15

List of Reports from the Committee of Public Accounts Session 2005–06 16

Summary

Implementation of previous recommendations

The net cost of the 2001 Foot and Mouth epidemic to the taxpayer was approximately £2.7 billion (gross cost £3 billion). The epidemic was one of the largest and most costly animal disease outbreaks ever recorded, with at least six million animals slaughtered. The European Commission disallowed £610 million of the UK's claim of £960 million for reimbursement of the costs of the outbreak. Our predecessors reported on the Department for Environment, Food and Rural Affairs' ("the Department") handling of the 2001 outbreak in its Report published in March 2003.[1]

The Department has made good progress in implementing most of our predecessors' recommendations. In particular, the Department has:

- improved its animal health policies to reduce the risk of a further outbreak.

- strengthened its preparedness through enhanced contingency planning, by increasing the number of veterinarians and other resources needed to handle an outbreak, and by banning some animal feeds and limiting animal movements to prevent rapid spread of the disease.

- clarified its approach to the use of vaccinations in any future outbreak.

- tightened its procedures for valuing commercial animals.

Further action is required, however, in two key areas:

a) Controlling the cost of a future outbreak

Procedures for valuing pedigree and high value stock continue to rely solely on valuer judgement. The reasonableness of completed assessments should be validated by comparison to other relevant documentation such as original purchase price, and valuations should be benchmarked for consistency and fairness.

The Department has yet to complete discussions with the industry about a proposed animal disease levy through which parties would share the cost and responsibility for dealing with future outbreaks. A levy system which linked contributions to standards of biosecurity could benefit the sector as well as the taxpayer. Additionally, the Department has yet to resolve whether the cost of disinfection and cleaning should be funded by the taxpayer, by the industry or be shared.

---

1   5th Report from the Committee of Public Accounts, *The 2001 outbreak of Foot and Mouth Disease,* (HC 487, Session 2002–03)

b) Managing Future Outbreaks

The Department's and other parties' contingency plans, such as those of local authorities, need to be current and consistent to facilitate co-ordination and co-operation in a future outbreak. To reduce the risk of future outbreaks, farmers' compliance with animal health standards should be subject to enhanced scrutiny on a risk assessment basis. The Department should establish adequate Information Technology systems to assist in the management of future disease outbreaks.

On the basis of a further Report by the Comptroller and Auditor General,[2] our predecessors took evidence from the Department on its progress in controlling and sharing the costs of a further outbreak, preparedness for a future epidemic, and disease control options such as vaccination and culling.

---

2   C&AG's Report, *Foot and Mouth: applying the lessons* (HC 184, Session 2004–05)

Conclusions and recommendations

1. **The Department has tightened controls over the payment of compensation to farmers for slaughtered animals** through appointing an approved list of valuers, remunerating valuers on an hourly basis rather than a percentage of the valuation, and using average price data from the Meat and Livestock Commission to inform valuations.

2. **For non-standard and pedigree animals, however, the Department still relies on professional valuations, even though experience from 2001 suggests some valuations were two to three times the underlying worth of the animal.** The Department should seek to substantiate such valuations by reference to other relevant data, for example original purchase price or values for similar animals in different parts of the country. It should challenge, and expect the farmer or valuer to justify, any unusual movements.

3. **Implementation of a levy scheme could transfer part or all of the cost of future disease outbreaks from the taxpayer to farmers**, as is the case already for arable farmers. A levy scheme could also provide incentives to improve farm biosecurity, for example by linking the amount of levy contribution to standards of biosecurity maintained on a farm. The Department should make quick progress on consultation on such a scheme, and should resolve quickly the question of transferring to the industry the costs of secondary disinfection of farms.

4. **Weak financial controls operated by the Department during the 2001 outbreak have made it difficult for the Department to substantiate and settle contractors' invoices, some of which are now four years old.** The Department should set a deadline for completion of its detailed forensic audit work and for settling all outstanding claims.

5. **Targeting inspections increasingly on a risk assessment basis would reduce risks of a future disease outbreak.** Inspectors having and applying a comprehensive and clear understanding of all relevant legislation and regulations is also essential. The Department should enhance the effectiveness of its inspection regime by greater co-ordination, co-operation and information sharing with local authority staff and through use of peer-review, quality checks, and training to encourage strict application of animal health regulations.

6. **Good biosecurity should be encouraged through effective deterrents for those farmers who fail to meet minimum standards thereby putting at risk their own and others' livelihoods.** The Department has limited data on the outcome of local authority prosecutions, or the size of fines imposed by courts. The Department should identify and collect the necessary data and consider whether it would be appropriate to ask the Sentencing Advisory Council to frame a sentencing guideline on breaches of farm biosecurity.

7. **The Department will need first class project management skills to control a future outbreak effectively, ultimate success being dependent on effective co-ordination with local authorities, emergency services and other stakeholders.** The

Department has put in place an enhanced contingency plan with clear management responsibilities allocated for operations and finance. The Department should establish a timetable for relevant local bodies to produce contingency plans, and for testing such plans alongside its central plan, in scenarios ranging from accidental to deliberate introduction of diseases.

8. **The Department has now clarified its policy and approach to the use of vaccination and/or a contiguous cull to eradicate future disease outbreaks.** This approach is being underpinned by a cost benefit analysis of the effectiveness of different disease control options. The Department should meet its commitment to put the report in the public domain quickly.

1 Controlling and sharing the costs of a further epidemic

1. Compensation for slaughtered animals accounted for £1.4 billion of the cost of the 2001 outbreak. The European Commission disallowed some 60% of the UK's claim for reimbursement of compensation costs, agreeing to pay only £254 million of the £652 million claimed.[3] The Commission considered that there had been poor control over compensation arrangements and it estimated that payments to UK farmers were around two to three times the true value of the animals slaughtered. The Department's approach in 2001 had been based on controlling overall costs by rapid eradication of the disease.

2. For the future, the Department intended to appoint livestock valuers from an approved national list, paid by the hour rather than as a percentage of the valuations, with four "monitor" valuers to quality assure the valuers' work. The Department had also issued detailed instructions on how valuations should be undertaken. The Department was introducing standard valuations and compensation for animals (including cattle) slaughtered for other types of animal disease, but would need new primary legislation to do so for Foot and Mouth. The Meat and Livestock Commission would, however, disseminate market information to valuers to inform the valuation of standard animals. The difficulties of validating the reasonableness of valuations placed on pedigree and other valuable animals remained.[4]

3. The Department no longer planned to pay compensation for animals slaughtered on welfare grounds although it would pay for the cost of disposal. It considered farmers to be responsible for their animals, and for feeding them, and its current contingency plan made provision for licensed movements to ease welfare problems.[5]

4. The European Commission had disallowed 80% of UK expenditure on the cleansing and disinfection of farms affected by the outbreak. In dealing with the 2001 outbreak the Department could have required farmers to meet the cost of cleaning and disinfecting farms. Instead, the Department reimbursed farmers at an average cost of £30,000 a farm. This approach had led, in the Department's view, to a thorough and consistent process, reducing the likelihood of re-infection, and it remained current policy. Whether the cost should be passed on to farmers would be part of its consultation exercise on an animal disease levy.[6]

5. Four years after the end of the 2001 Foot and Mouth epidemic, the Department had still not settled extended contractual disputes with 76 contractors who had claimed some £40 million. The poor financial controls over expenditure, highlighted in our

---

3   The UK's claim of £960 million comprised £652 million in respect of compensation for slaughtered animals and £308 million for other costs.

4   Qq 2–3, 50–52, 66–68

5   Qq 39–40

6   Qq 57–60, 108–109

predecessors' Report, contributed to the Department's difficulties in verifying sums claimed. The Department has put in place new contracting arrangements for future outbreaks, including contingency contracts and prearranged prices to reduce the scope for contractual disputes.[7]

6. The Department confirmed its intention to bring forward proposals for sharing the cost of outbreaks in its Animal Health and Welfare Strategy published in 2004. It intended to consider the issue as part of a more general review of the regulation of charging in the farming sector more generally. Consultation on the broader agenda would take place later in 2005. The Department had been unsuccessful in its initial plans to link the amount of compensation payable to the standards of biosecurity maintained by the farmer. In the Department's view, biosecurity could not be assessed objectively. The Department was, however, considering proposals for an animal disease levy to share the future costs of disease outbreaks with the industry. Standards of poor biosecurity might be taken into account in such a scheme, for example through lower charges for those farmers with better biosecurity.

7   Qq 13, 48, 62–65

2 Preparations for a future epidemic

7. In the Department's view an outbreak of foot and mouth disease could not be entirely prevented as the risk of diseased meat getting into the country could not be eliminated. Robust animal health inspection regimes were critical to reducing the risk of future outbreaks of serious contagious diseases and to raising animal husbandry standards. Departmental inspectors require a sound understanding of the technical and legislative environment to underpin their risk assessments of farms and to adopt a more rigorous approach to maintaining standards of public and animal health. The Department was undertaking targeted inspections co-ordinated between local government and the State Veterinary Service. The risk based approach took account of the nature and scale of businesses, local knowledge, animal density levels, and the number of animal movements.[8]

8. The maximum penalty for breaches of biosecurity is imprisonment for up to 2 years and/or an unlimited fine.[9] Responsibility for prosecuting breaches of biosecurity lies with local authorities. The Department did not routinely collect data on the number of prosecutions or their outcomes. Outcomes for two local authority areas, North Yorkshire (12 cases) and Cumbria (3 cases), indicated, however, that the Courts had imposed modest penalties **(Figure 1)**.[10]

Figure 1: Prosecutions for serious breaches of biosecurity procedures in North Yorkshire and Cumbria from September 2001 to May 2002

Outcome	Number of prosecutions
12 month conditional discharge	2
£100 fine plus costs	5 (6 offences)
£200 fine plus costs	2 (3 offences)
£225 fine plus costs	1 (2 offences)
£250 fine plus costs	2
£300 fine	1
£300 fine plus costs	2 (3 offences)

Source: National Audit Office analysis of supplementary written evidence (Ev 23)

9. Restrictions on sheep and cattle movements introduced after the 2001 outbreak had reduced the spread of disease. Spot checks on traffic to identify the illegal transportation of animals had also been effective. The State Veterinary Service had access to a web-

---

8   Qq 19–20, 29, 70–74

9   Animal Health Act 1981 and related legislation

10   Ev 23

based secure enforcement database used by trading standards staff in 170 local authorities in England and Wales to record enforcement action for breaches of livestock movements. The Department was, however, only aware of the outcome in 69 of the 191 prosecutions initiated in 2003, which comprised 58 convictions, 9 cases withdrawn and 2 subject to appeal. It had no specific information on the level of fines imposed by courts although it noted that the data should be held by the prosecuting local authority.[11]

10. The Department considered that it was better prepared for a future outbreak. It had appointed six senior civil servants to take charge of the disease control operation as Regional Operations Directors. Eight further staff had been appointed as Divisional Operations Managers and a further seven as finance managers. Military liaison officers would be appointed to each National and Local disease control centre. The Department could however do more to encourage the preparation of linked local authority, emergency services, tourist industry and other rural stakeholder plans, and to conduct joint exercises. Linking and joint testing the contingency plans of all the parties involved in responding to an outbreak would help facilitate a more immediate national co-ordinated response.[12]

11. The Departments' contingency plan took account of the risk of deliberate introduction of the disease, including the risk that a number of different strains might be introduced. Early diagnosis, laboratory facilities and vaccination antigens would help tackle such a situation.[13] Farm health plans were a major initiative in the Department's Animal Health and Welfare strategy, and a working party had been set up to look at sharing best practice. Poster and advertising campaigns had been used to address, for example, biosecurity in markets.[14]

12. The National Contingency plan included a communication strategy which required daily engagement with stakeholders at a local level. 24 hour phone numbers were in place, and senior staff were being trained to deal with media questions. Exercise Hornby had been carried out in the summer of 2004 to simulate an outbreak and test plans. The Department had improved its information systems since the outbreak of 2001. On the advice of its consultants, however, it had delayed the introduction of its enhanced web-based database system until underlying problems had been resolved. Work to integrate the new database and the State Veterinary Service Agency's information technology programme was continuing. In the meantime, the Department's existing system was to be upgraded to provide support.[15]

---

11   Qq 76, 82–85; Ev 22–23

12   C&AG's Report, para 3.4; Qq 9, 30–33

13   Q 79

14   Qq 10–11, 58, 61, 68, 186–187

15   Qq 34–35, 80, 136

3 Vaccination or cull

13. The contiguous cull of 2001 remains highly controversial as healthy animals may have been slaughtered. The Department had commissioned a major cost benefit analysis looking at four different disease control strategies, including a contiguous cull. The results were expected to be made publicly available but were currently waiting peer and other expert review.

14. The Department had set out its likely response to a future outbreak. The first line of disease control would still be the slaughter of susceptible animals on infected premises and dangerous contacts in line with European Union requirements. Depending on the circumstances, the Department would then consider using a policy of vaccination to live, making use of the Decision Tree **(Figure 2)** developed as part of its contingency plan. The Department had no plans for a repetition of the mass funeral pyres used to dispose of carcasses in the 2001 outbreak.[16]

16   Qq 14, 18, 123–124

Figure 2: The Decision Tree showing the factors influencing the decision of when to vaccinate animals

Factors influencing the decision of when to vaccinate animals have been set out by the Department in a Decision Tree included in the Foot and Mouth Disease contingency plan

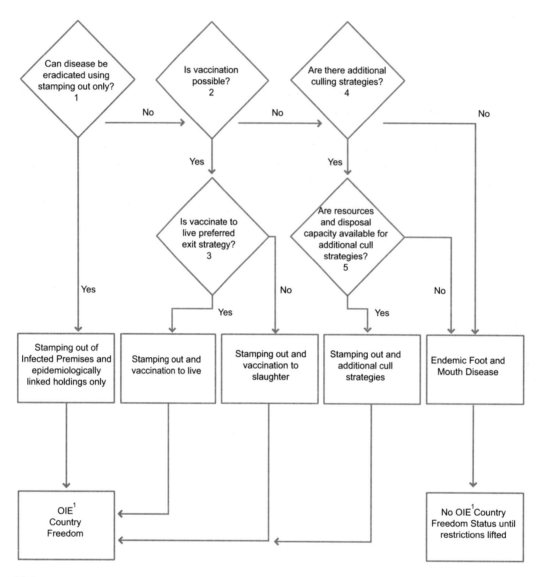

Note:

1 The Office International des Epizooties (OIE) determines the disease status of countries for the purpose of international trade in animal products.

Source: Department for Environment, Food and Rural Affairs' Foot and Mouth Disease Contingency Plan, Annex D, December 2003

15. The Department needed to educate consumers about alternatives to culling, including vaccination to live and vaccination to die. Vaccination was not used in 2001 partly because of the actual and anticipated farmer and consumer resistance to meat from vaccinated animals. Too little information had been made available to the public, farmers and supermarkets about the effects of vaccination on public health, and about the impact of vaccination on the export status of UK beef. Meat from animals vaccinated against other diseases was already on sale in the UK. Individual farmers might still need to be persuaded, however, as might retailers and consumers. The Department confirmed that it had legal powers under a Statutory Instrument to vaccinate in a vaccination zone even if farmers objected. The National Farmers Union supported the use of vaccination.[17]

16. The Department had practical arrangements in place to enable it to vaccinate infected cattle within five days of disease confirmation. A range of vaccines covering nine different strains of the disease were available. As an outbreak could result from more than one virus strain, the Department also had access to vaccines covering other strains held elsewhere in the European Union.[18]

---

17 Qq 42–44, 93–104, 127–135

18 Q 42

Formal minutes

Monday 17 October 2005

Members present:

Mr Edward Leigh, in the Chair

Mr Richard Bacon   Jon Trickett
Mr Greg Clark   Kitty Ussher
Ms Diana R Johnson

Draft Report (Foot and Mouth Disease: applying the lessons), proposed by the Chairman, brought up and read.

Ordered, That the draft Report be read a second time, paragraph by paragraph.

Paragraphs 1 to 16 read and agreed to.

Conclusions and recommendations read and agreed to.

Summary read and agreed to.

Resolved, That the Report be the Ninth Report of the Committee to the House.

Ordered, That the Chairman do make the Report to the House.

Ordered, That the provisions of Standing Order No. 134 (Select Committees (Reports)) be applied to the Report.

[Adjourned until Wednesday 19 October at 3.30 pm

Witnesses

Wednesday 23 February 2005   *Page*

**Sir Brian Bender KCB, Dr Debby Reynolds, Ms Glenys Stacey, Mr Simon
Hewitt, Mr David Rabey,** Department for Environment, Food and Rural Affairs,
and **Mr Barney Holbeche,** National Farmers' Union   Ev 1

List of written evidence

Department for Environment, Food and Rural Affairs   Ev 20
National Farmers' Union   Ev 24
Map of Burnside Farm, submitted by the Department for Environment, Food and
    Rural Affairs   Ev 26

List of Reports from the Committee of Public Accounts
Session 2005–06

First Report	Managing National Lottery Distribution Fund balances	HC 408
Second Report	The regeneration of the Millennium Dome and associated land	HC 409
Third Report	Ministry of Defence: Major Projects Report 2004	HC 410
Fourth Report	Fraud and error in benefit expenditure	HC 411
Fifth Report	Inland Revenue: Tax Credits and deleted tax cases	HC 412
Sixth Report	Department of Trade and Industry: Renewable energy	HC 413
Seventh Report	The use of operating theatres in the Northern Ireland Health and Personal Social Services	HC 414
Eighth Report	Navan Centre	HC 415
Ninth Report	Foot and Mouth Disease: applying the lessons	HC 563

The reference number of the Treasury Minute to each Report will be printed in brackets after the HC printing number

Oral evidence

Taken before the Committee of Public Accounts

on Wednesday 23 February 2005

Members present:

Mr Edward Leigh, in the Chair

Mrs Angela Browning	Mr Brian Jenkins
Mr David Curry	Mr Gerry Steinberg
Mr Ian Davidson	Mr Alan Williams

Sir John Bourn, Comptroller and Auditor General, National Audit Office, further examined.

Mr Brian Glicksman CB, Treasury Officer of Accounts, HM Treasury, further examined.

REPORT BY THE COMPTROLLER AND AUDITOR GENERAL:

Department for Environment, Food and Rural Affairs: Foot and Mouth Disease: applying the lessons (HC 184)

Witnesses: **Sir Brian Bender KCB,** Permanent Secretary, **Dr Debby Reynolds,** Chief Veterinary Officer and Director General for Animal Health and Welfare, **Ms Glenys Stacey,** Chief Executive Designate of the State Veterinary Service, **Mr Simon Hewitt,** Head of Exotic Diseases Prevention and Control Division, **Mr David Rabey,** Director of Purchasing, Department for Environment, Food and Rural Affairs, and **Mr Barney Holbeche,** Head of Parliamentary Affairs, National Farmers' Union, examined.

Q1 Chairman: Welcome to the Committee of Public Accounts. Before I start the meeting I am afraid our Committee Assistant, Leslie Young, is leaving us so I would like to thank her on behalf of the Committee for all her sterling work she has done. We are dealing today with a very serious subject, the Foot and Mouth outbreak, applying the lessons. We are joined, once again, by Sir Brian Bender, who is the Permanent Secretary at the Department for the Environment, Food and Rural Affairs. You are very welcome back to our Committee. Would you like to introduce your colleagues, please.
Sir Brian Bender: Thank you, Chairman. On my right is Dr Debby Reynolds who is Chief Veterinary Officer. She took over the job in March of last year. On my left is Glenys Stacey, who has been appointed to become the Chief Executive of the State Veterinary Service. She is in post now and will become the Chief Executive on 1 April.

Q2 Chairman: Thank you, Sir Brian. Could I start by asking you about compensation. If you refer to paragraphs 4.2 and 4.5, which you can find on pages 29 and 30, you will recall that the Members of this Committee did issue a Report in March 2003. We were very keen on using benchmarks for compensation or typical market values to inform the valuers' decisions. Now, why do your interim arrangements not accept this?
Sir Brian Bender: We have appointed monitor valuers. We have a list of valuers, and the Report describes that, which I will come back to if the Committee asks. On the question of whether or not

we have benchmarks, we are out to consultation at the moment, and we are producing standard values for disease in cattle where we do not need primary legislation, and that includes TB and BSE. In the case of Foot and Mouth Disease, we would need primary legislation to have standard compensation. In terms of benchmarks, the fundamental issue is where there is no market, such as for pedigree animals and some others, it is difficult to identify, as the Report says, how we would have a benchmark. Where there is a market, our intention is to ensure that the Meat and Livestock Commission disseminates market information to the valuers as effectively as possible.

Q3 Chairman: When you get your legislation you are going to use benchmarks, are you not?
Sir Brian Bender: Our intention is to have much more standard values and compensation values. As I say, at the moment we are intending to implement it for the cattle diseases which do not require primary legislation from the end of this year.

Q4 Chairman: If you look at paragraph 20, which you can find on page six, which deals with the final cost of the 2001 epidemic, you will see in the middle there that the European Commission concluded "... that farmers were compensated on average between two and three times the market value". You know that you put in a claim for £960 million, did you not?

DEFRA and NFU

Sir Brian Bender: Correct.

Q5 Chairman: Instead they agreed to pay £350 million?
Sir Brian Bender: Correct.

Q6 Chairman: That is a £600 million loss to the British taxpayer. How can you explain the slap in the face and this grotesque waste of public money?
Sir Brian Bender: There are a number of aspects to that, Chairman, if I may. The first, as I said at the hearing this Committee had in 2002, is that the decision taken at the time was that rapid eradication of the disease, in what was an unprecedented outbreak, was the best approach to keep overall costs down. Secondly, in fact the Commission have always historically been very strict on paying claims. For example, in their classical swine fever outbreak in 1997 the Dutch received only 28% of their claim.

Q7 Chairman: The fact that other people may have also failed to do this job properly is no excuse, surely. If you are going to apply for money to the Commission, does it not make sense to at least carry out your compensation arrangements in such a way that you might have some chance of receiving compensation on the behalf of British taxpayers?
Sir Brian Bender: Chairman, again, if I may, two aspects there. First of all, the Commission themselves produced a table of alleged over-valuation of animals where our alleged over-valuation of cattle was less than that in Ireland, France and the Netherlands. Secondly, there are lessons from how it applied last time.

Q8 Chairman: You are in favour of benchmarks in comparing yourselves to other countries but not—
Sir Brian Bender: What I am trying to say is that everybody—according to the Commission—over-valued. However, the other point is there are plainly lessons in how we applied financial controls last time. The Committee made some telling points in its Report after the last hearing and we believe we have learned those and are applying them looking forward.

Q9 Chairman: The head of the Civil Service tells us that the new buzz word in Whitehall is project management. Your project management was pretty weak here, in fact you had virtually no contingency plan at all apparently.
Sir Brian Bender: Again, the Committee had exhaustive discussion of this last time. We did have a contingency plan. Clearly it was not adequate for what we had to face. We believe, now, and the NAO Report says, that we are now much better prepared—and I believe we are—in a number of areas, including financial controls.

Q10 Chairman: Okay. Let us look at the future. I want to ask you about sharing the cost of outbreaks. This is dealt with in paragraph 4.9, which you will find on page 31. You may remember that you promised us that you would bring forward proposals

for sharing the cost of outbreaks in the summer of 2003. It is now winter 2005—February 2005—why have these proposals not seen the light of day?
Sir Brian Bender: The principle was reconfirmed in the Animal Health and Welfare Strategy we published last year. The policy decision that has been taken is that the issue should be approached in the context of an overview of regulation of charging in the farming sector, and not simply taken in isolation. What we are doing is working on that overview and our intention is to go out to consultation on it later this year.

Q11 Chairman: I want to deal now with farmers who are guilty of poor husbandry. You can find reference to this on pages 30 to 31 and paragraphs 4.6 to 4.8. Why do you not take poor husbandry on the part of an individual farmer into account in determining a levy on farmers?
Sir Brian Bender: As the Committee may know, we tried to put a requirement in the Animal Health Act to do this and because of the strong opposition at the time the Government withdrew that provision. What we are looking at now is, indeed, this issue in the context of the animal disease levy, in other words whether there will be some form of shared cost or, in terms of farm health planning, a lower charge for farmers that have either worse biosecurity on the one hand or better biosecurity on the other. It is on the table but not in the form that we were looking at two or three years ago.

Q12 Chairman: Because, of course, Mr Waugh's farm in Northumberland where the outbreak started, it was a filthy farm, he got compensation, did he not?
Sir Brian Bender: He got compensation for slaughtered animals because there was a legal requirement. He also got a sentence from the courts.

Q13 Chairman: I want to ask you now about the delay in settling contractors' invoices. You can find reference to this at paragraph 21, page six. How can you justify the fact, Sir Brian, that you still have not paid all your bills? There is still £40 million outstanding.
Sir Brian Bender: Chairman, I would justify it by virtue of my responsibility to protect taxpayers' money because these are not agreed and accepted accounts where the money is outstanding; these are disputed accounts and we have had teams of accountants, lawyers, forensic people looking at the quantum, looking at the volume and seeking to engage with the individual people. There is a slight update on the data in the Report. The number of contractors whose final settlement is agreed has gone up from 73 to 76 in table 12. This position is moving. There are a number of cases currently before the courts. We do not wish to litigate if we can avoid it but the delay is not a wish to delay making due payments, far from it; the delay arises where we believe on the best advice we have there is not sufficient evidence that the claim is justified and then we are trying to resolve those cases individually.

Q14 Chairman: You will know, I am sure we are agreed, one of the most distressing aspects of the last outbreak were these mass pyres that we saw with the animals being burnt. Can you give me an assurance now that in future you will have sufficient incineration and landfill capacity?

Sir Brian Bender: The Government has stated in its contingency plan it is not the intention to use pyres again, except possibly in remote areas like the Highlands, and it is not the intention to use mass burial sites. As the Report describes, there is a hierarchy of disposal that begins with incineration and rendering; for a larger outbreak we would need to use licensed landfill.

Q15 Chairman: I think it is a very brave pledge you are giving us but we take it.

Sir Brian Bender: It is the Government's stated policy.

Chairman: It does not militate against the fact it is a brave pledge.

Mr Steinberg: Brave Government.

Q16 Chairman: Lastly, disease control strategies, you have got a cost-benefit analysis coming up soon, have you not?

Sir Brian Bender: Correct.

Q17 Chairman: You have commissioned, when will it be available please?

Sir Brian Bender: It will be available to the Department in the next very few weeks. It will need to be peer reviewed then but we intend to publish it in the light of the peer review. I would not like to put a firm date on that, but soon.

Q18 Chairman: Are you prepared to share anything from that report about the impact and effectiveness of a contiguous cull? Again, this was one of the most distressing parts of the outbreak.

Sir Brian Bender: The cost-benefit analysis is going to look at four different scenarios, one of which would be a contiguous cull. There is a separate issue which I think this Report—the NAO Report—refers to, of the way different epidemiological experts have examined the data on the 2001 outbreak and reached different views on the value of a contiguous cull. The Government does not rule out a contiguous cull in the future but it would not be the preferred approach. The EU Directive requires slaughter on infected premises and dangerous contacts, and then the next stage would be whether or not vaccination can be part of the armoury.

Q19 Mrs Browning: Sir Brian, this outbreak has cost £3 billion of which £1.4 billion has been the cost of the animals which were culled during the outbreak. For those of us who represent rural seats, such as mine in Devon, we all know that there is a somewhat more unquantifiable cost in terms of what this did to the farming community. Could I draw your attention to page 14, which is right at the beginning of the Report. Could I ask you, first, do you think Defra could have been prevented this outbreak?

Sir Brian Bender: Prevented the outbreak in 2001, no. The risk of diseased meat getting into the country can never be reduced to zero. We believe that we have improved control since then. The risk of the diseased meat reaching animals, susceptible species, can never be reduced to zero; but through things like the swill controls we believe we have reduced that risk significantly. The risk of the disease being in a herd and spreading depends on the biosecurity of farmers and also some of the controls we have introduced, such as the six day standstill. We believe we have seriously reduced the risks but I do not think in 2001 we could have prevented it. I think it would be extremely brave for me to sit before this Committee and say, "We would prevent any outbreak in the future".

Q20 Mrs Browning: Could you just refamiliarise yourself with paragraph 2.3 which sets out the genesis of the lamb imported from Argentina coming in and its inclusion in pigswill. It says here ". . . the failure of a farmer to heat-treat the swill to inactivate the virus. The feeding of swill to pigs was rare in 2001 and since May 2001 has been banned. Farms are subject to a range of inspections both by the Department and local authorities." Sir Brian, are you aware that Bobby Waugh, whose farm was identified as the index case for Foot and Mouth in 2001, was contravening Article 21(2) of the Animal Byproducts Order 1999 at Burnside Farm?

Sir Brian Bender: I am conscious that there were issues around what was going on on his farm and, indeed, there were periodic visits and inspections of his farm. The most recent inspection, which was in January 2001, happened to be before we believe there was any virus present but I do not think that was your question. The question was whether presumably there was anything that should have been done at the time of that or previous visits.

Q21 Mrs Browning: Yes?

Sir Brian Bender: Hindsight is a wonderful thing. I do not know whether the Chief Vet would like to comment on this?

Dr Reynolds: Only to say that hindsight is a wonderful thing and risk assessment by the Veterinary Laboratories Agency does show a great deal of uncertainty on the potential for both illegal imports of meat and particularly around those which might be infected. That is why stopping the swill feeding route of exposure to pigs which could get the virus so seriously, was a very important step that was taken during 2001.

Q22 Mrs Browning: It was not just as it says here, and as I have seen reported elsewhere, the feeding of this unprocessed swill to pigs, it was the very fact that under your Ministry's own Article 21(2) of the Animal Byproducts Order, it was not just a question of feeding, it was a matter of having unprocessed waste on the premises at all where pigs and other ruminants are kept.

Sir Brian Bender: There are plainly issues about how effectively, first of all, farmers who have a responsibility themselves, obey the law and, secondly, how effectively our risk based inspection arrangements are. We believe they are better now as a result of various bits of data but undoubtedly in a perfect world this would not have happened because the issues would have been spotted.

Q23 Mrs Browning: Are you aware that the State Veterinary Officer, Jim Dring, made a signed submission to Anderson's Lessons Learned Inquiry in which he admits that he was aware that Mr Bobbie Waugh was bringing unprocessed catering waste on to Burnside Farm prior to the outbreak of Foot and Mouth Disease in 2001?
Sir Brian Bender: I am very aware of Jim Dring's statement. It was not a submission to the Anderson Inquiry but he did produce a personal statement. In fact, there has been some discussion with Dr Anderson because Dr Anderson did not see that at the time. Nonetheless, Jim Dring did make such a statement and again he was applying, if you like, personal hindsight to the situation. Obviously what happened is regrettable. In a perfect world perhaps this issue would have been spotted and a disease outbreak would not have happened. The question is how we can learn the lessons from that for our inspection arrangements which are shared between the State Veterinary Service and local authorities to try and stop that happening in future.

Q24 Mrs Browning: It would have been a requirement to inspect every six months to renew an Article 26 licence on Burnside Farm?
Sir Brian Bender: Yes.
Mr Hewitt: For feeders of swill it was a six month inspection.

Q25 Mrs Browning: Yes. What I would ask you then is do you accept now that Jim Dring failed to fulfil his regulatory duties under the Animal Byproducts Order 1999 by allowing Bobby Waugh not just to feed the unprocessed swill to his pigs but by bringing unprocessed catering waste on to Burnside Farm at all?
Sir Brian Bender: I am very happy to provide the Committee with a note on that. I have not come prepared with sufficient information, to be fair either to Mrs Browning asking the question or, indeed, to Mr Dring in the way I respond to it. I am very happy to provide the Committee with a note afterwards. I apologise for not being able to answer it now.[1]

Q26 Mrs Browning: If you are unable to answer it now and you write to us, would you take a look also at whether you think it was down to Mr Dring personally, who clearly made that written statement to the Anderson Inquiry? I am very focused on this Byproducts Order because it is not just, as people tend to talk about, feeding to pigs, it is the actual presence of catering waste on the farm at all which was in contravention of the Order. I would ask you whether you accept that there was negligence within

the management structure of the State Veterinary Service which allowed Mr Dring's work to go unmonitored?
Sir Brian Bender: I understand the question, I will cover this in the note.

Q27 Mrs Browning: Will you let us know whether you accept that the SVS accept responsibility for Mr Dring's actions?
Sir Brian Bender: I will cover that. The SVS then and now certainly would accept responsibility. That is the role of managers.

Q28 Mrs Browning: That will be clear in your written note?
Sir Brian Bender: I will cover this point and look carefully at the transcript.

Q29 Mrs Browning: The reason I am very focused on this—you will be aware that there have been many parliamentary questions, of which I myself have put down questions and correspondence with ministers on this—it comes back to the question I asked you originally whether you felt DEFRA could have prevented this. Yes, we are talking about lessons learned, and I come back to that paragraph 2.3 at the beginning of this where it states ". . . The feeding of swill to pigs was rare in 2001 . . .". That may well be the case but it was not just the feeding of swill, it was the presence of that catering waste in contravention of a DEFRA regulation. What I am really asking you is if DEFRA had managed to uphold its own regulations could they have prevented the Foot and Mouth outbreak occurring?
Sir Brian Bender: Again, I will cover this in the note. My view is in a perfect world that may have been the case. The question looking forward is whether through a combination of the work we are doing on biosecurity, on targeted risk of enforcement and on farm health plans, we will minimise these risks in the future because one can never reduce them to zero, we do not live in that sort of perfect world.
Mrs Browning: It may not be a perfect world, Sir Brian, but personally I sat through a two year public inquiry and I have to tell you nobody ever prayed in aid "it is not a perfect world" when they investigated BSE. I hope you will take that on board when you make your written submission to the Chairman. Thank you.

Q30 Mr Curry: Sir Brian, if there was to be an outbreak of Foot and Mouth Disease in the Pennine Dales of Yorkshire, who would be put in charge of dealing with it?
Sir Brian Bender: From day one we would establish a Regional Operations Director in the local Disease Control Centre to whom, for administration and management purposes, the local veterinary service would work. The veterinary judgments would not be overseen but the operations would be. We would bring in also a military liaison officer on day one into the local disease centre to work with the civilians and liaise with the MoD as to whether or not it was appropriate to bring in the army.

Q31 Mr Curry: Who is the person who would do that job?
Sir Brian Bender: We have a list of volunteer Regional Operations Directors, members of the Senior Civil Service, who receive a certain period of training each year and who would step in. Two or three of them did that role in the exercise last summer.

Q32 Mr Curry: Where is the regional centre they would operate from in this case?
Sir Brian Bender: Probably Leeds. You will recall, probably even better than I, in the 2001 outbreak we opened, in effect, a sub-office because of the geography when the outbreak happened.

Q33 Mr Curry: The reason I ask the question is that in the last outbreak one had the impression that nobody was in charge, and certainly nobody was in charge of the vets. The vets were not within the overall management structure. You had Antipodean vets racing around North Yorkshire on a variety of missions. You had nobody in charge of the overall management. One of the things which struck me forcibly afterwards was the State Veterinary Service simply had to be brought under the overall management control of the Department, they could not be allowed to function like a semi-autonomous organisation. Are you satisfied that the vets are now under control, as it were?
Sir Brian Bender: They are under control directly of a lawyer. That is not an entirely facetious response. The Chief Executive Designate, who is the senior leader and manager of vets is, in fact, a lawyer by training not a vet. My more serious answer to the question is that the various changes that we made during Foot and Mouth last time but would apply from day one next time would be intended to have an integrated management structure. We did not put the Regional Operations Directors in place until several weeks into the outbreak.

Q34 Mr Curry: You ended up with an effective system and high quality people in charge. A lot had got by before that happened. One of the things which got by was the great difficulty of making contact. You had various phone numbers for emergencies which never, ever were answered, no-one could ever get through. What measures have you put in place to make sure that communication between the direct and regional centre is always accessible?
Ms Stacey: There is a communication strategy now.

Q35 Mr Curry: Not depending on websites, please. Farmers in my constituency do not always have them.
Ms Stacey: There is a communication strategy set out as part of the national contingency plan for managing Foot and Mouth Disease and other such diseases. It requires at a local level daily engagement with stakeholders, for example, so you have daily meetings where the up-to-the-minute picture is exchanged. There are also now 24 hour phone numbers to contact which are local phone numbers.

It should be possible for us to manage both phone and direct stakeholder communication on a daily basis.

Q36 Mr Curry: One of the things which struck me during the last outbreak was that the regional directors when they were in place obviously had to be exposed to the media but they were, by definition, being exposed to a great deal of what you might call political questioning. They were required to answer questions which really should be directed towards their political masters. How does one deal with this topic?
Sir Brian Bender: I do not think there is a simple answer because I think the senior official on the spot, who would be a Regional Operations Director, will need to deal with local stakeholders, as Glenys Stacey said, and different media and, therefore, will need to learn how to handle as a civil servant the difficult questions, as indeed the Chief Vet did last time.

Q37 Mr Curry: Are they getting trained in that?
Sir Brian Bender: Yes.

Q38 Mr Curry: Are you doing war games with them?
Sir Brian Bender: They are having that sort of media training and, indeed, some of the state vets had last time apparently.

Q39 Mr Curry: Could we move on to the welfare culling. The most profligate area of public expenditure was probably the welfare cull because anything with four legs which was capable of showing signs of a heartbeat then did receive a vast amount of compensation payment without question from a terribly overwhelmed Newcastle office, speaking from personal experience. You have gone now from the position where in practice things were signed off really without question to saying you are not going to pay compensation at all, you are going to rely on other mechanisms. Do you think that is a fair balance to have arrived at and how confident are you the other mechanisms will work given that, as you have admitted and we all accept, the urgency last time was to get farmer co-operation pretty damn quick at almost whatever price?
Sir Brian Bender: We believe, as it were, as part of the overall more rapid response, a more effective response is in place and, as you know, the policy is that the cost of disposal should be paid for by the taxpayer, but not any compensation for the cost of the lost livestock. All this is against the background that it is the farmers' responsibility fundamentally to look after their animals and feed them.

Q40 Mr Curry: Yes, but hang on, last time the reason why there was a welfare problem was farmers could not do that. They were sucking the stones dry. They could not move their animals. People got caught on the pastures, could not be brought home, could not be moved. There may well have been some which did not but on the whole we were trying to mitigate the problems not cause the problems.

DEFRA and NFU

Sir Brian Bender: One of the issues plainly we have as part of our planning is the extent to which licensed movements can be eased to deal with the most pressing problems. This is not an easy area but I think one of the lessons certainly we felt last time was there had been an excessive expenditure of taxpayers' money on the welfare disposal, as, indeed, you said at the beginning of the question.

Q41 Mr Curry: Can I move on to vaccination. The starting point must be that we are only ever, I think, correct me if I am wrong, talking about vaccinating cattle, I do not think anyone is talking about vaccinating pigs or sheep?
Sir Brian Bender: Pigs at all? Sheep certainly not; I am not sure if pigs are ever a possibility but it is primarily cattle.
Dr Reynolds: It is primarily cattle, for a number of reasons. First of all, they are higher value animals and, secondly, it is possible to operate a vaccination campaign which is more likely to get ahead of the spread of the virus. Pigs produce so much more of the virus than other species, it is more legitimate to consider cattle for a vaccination campaign.

Q42 Mr Curry: Could I ask where we are on vaccination? There tends to be at large a feeling that there is a very simple choice, either you vaccinate or you slaughter. It is rather more complicated, is it not, because there are issues of diagnostic tests and the speed with which it works, there are issues about whether a vaccine can deal with the different strains of Foot and Mouth Disease, there is a question of whether you are vaccinating to live or vaccinating to die and there is a question of the status of the meat from the United Kingdom into the export markets if we are applying vaccination? Could you, without hesitation, deviation or repetition, in about one minute 43 seconds judging by this note, tell me where we are?
Sir Brian Bender: I will do my best. First of all, we have the practical arrangements in place to be able to vaccinate within five days of confirmation of a disease in terms of teams and systems in place. Secondly, plainly it depends on the strain of the virus. We have stocks of nine different strains and we have access to others through the EU bank.

Q43 Mr Curry: A diagnostic test which can identify the strain rapidly?
Sir Brian Bender: Yes. Whether or not we would vaccinate in a particular situation will depend on the nature of the outbreak. If we know where it is and we believe that it can be brought under control simply through slaughter on infected premises and dangerous contacts, we would not. We published a paper, which is available on our website, last summer that indicates the scenarios where certainly we would. The cost-benefit analysis we are doing will help inform that more. Certainly active consideration of vaccination to live would be high on the Government's priorities in the disease control policy in any outbreak.

Q44 Mr Curry: What about the question of the exportability of meat from the United Kingdom if we did pursue a vaccine to live policy? That was an issue, the status of the meat.
Sir Brian Bender: There are certain requirements on the way the meat needs to be treated. Subject to that, there should be no difficulty whatsoever within the EU. One can never have absolute guarantees about how third countries would react; and we have had a lot of meetings with stakeholders in the food chain, even the supermarkets, about their readiness to sell a vaccinated product without it creating a two-tier market.

Q45 Mr Curry: You mean without it being labelled?
Sir Brian Bender: Correct.

Q46 Mr Curry: They say they will do that, do they?
Sir Brian Bender: These discussions need to be pursued. So far they have been moderately reassuring.

Q47 Mr Curry: Personally I would much rather eat meat which had been fed GM crops than I would meat which had been vaccinated.
Sir Brian Bender: People from Argentina have been eating vaccinated meats for a long time.
Mr Curry: I will take your word on the dietary habits of the Argentineans. It is not a subject I have studied in great detail. I would like to come back with some other questions later, Chairman, if I may.

Q48 Mr Steinberg: It was mentioned earlier in the meeting that there were still people waiting for money to be paid to them. When I read this Report I felt as though not only should they not get that money but we should be getting some money back from those who were paid too much in the first place. In 2002 when we had the meeting, Sir Brian, you assured the Committee that the work the valuers had done was legitimate. Yet, if you go to page 35, paragraph 5.5, the European Commission, doing exactly what your Department should have done, at an early stage, found basically the opposite, did they not? I will read it out: "The Commission considered that the Department's poor control over the valuation process contributed towards higher than necessary compensation payments. The Commission examined a sample of 100 large compensation awards but found that the rationale for the valuation was largely absent from the files. Its enquiries with farmers and valuers produced explanations which the Commission found to be weak and unconvincing. Many of the farmers and valuers contacted by the Commission refused, or were unable, to provide documentary evidence to support claims of pedigree or high productivity". In other words, there was a huge fiddle going on, a gigantic fraud going on, and people were being paid literally hundreds of thousands of pounds of taxpayers' money and DEFRA just paid out.
Sir Brian Bender: I would not accept the words "fiddle" or "fraud".

Q49 Mr Steinberg: We will come to that.

Sir Brian Bender: I would refer you, Mr Steinberg, to the point I made earlier to the Chairman, that the data the Commission have produced indicates that the relative over-valuation that we provided for cattle was actually less than that in Ireland, France or the Netherlands. The figure for the UK under their data was 142%, France 159%, Netherlands 159% and Ireland 172%. The question, however, of course, is the arrangements left a lot to be desired.

Q50 Mr Steinberg: Could I just ask you, the policy at the time—correct me if I am wrong—was that the valuers were paid a percentage of the value of the stock, is that right?

Sir Brian Bender: They were. For the future, they are paid per hour.

Mr Steinberg: I rest my case. If you say to somebody "I am going to give you 10% of the value of so-and-so, now you go ahead and value it", my reaction is "I will take these for a fortune" which was exactly what they did, was it not? Look at figure 10, for example, just over the page. Remember these are the valuers who were getting a percentage of what they were valuing. Figure 10: "File No 12—the Commission queried the valuation of a bull, valued at £30,000 due to its advanced age—a nine year old".

Chairman: Are you valued at £30,000!

Q51 Mr Steinberg: I am a good old bull, I can tell you! I am a good breeding bull. "The maximum paid at auction for a prime bull in the UK prior to the outbreak was £42,000 . . ." Here was—what we would say in the North East—a hard bull that was ready which was paid £30,000 for. "Six rams purchased in October 2000 for an average of £60 were compensated at £535 per head . . ." I will miss the next one out. ". . . A farmer paid £14,000 for a yearling bull in January 2001. When slaughtered four months later, the bull was valued at £40,000". Are you telling me that the valuers were not taking you for a ride?

Sir Brian Bender: Two or three points on that. First of all, in some of these cases, for example the last one, we did look into it very carefully, the valuer said the valuation took two days and was done in an extremely thorough way. It was because the yearling was due to lay down a bank of semen for use in a champion herd. I am not defending, and I would not seek to defend, every single one of these cases. Can I just say looking forward, in terms of the controls, we have a list of valuers ourselves now who are approved by us in consultation with the trade associations.

Q52 Mr Steinberg: Were any of these valuers doing this before on the list?

Sir Brian Bender: I will come back to you on that.[2] We will be appointing the valuers, not the farmers. They will be paid by the hour not by any other form of commission. We have four monitor valuers who will be providing an oversight of what is happening.

Q53 Mr Steinberg: Basically, Sir Brian , I am saying they were fraudulent, you are saying that they were neglectful. Now in either case if they were fraudulent, as I think they were, they should be in court for a criminal action because they were thieving from the taxpayer, if they were neglectful then they should be in court for a civil action because they were incompetent in doing the job which cost the taxpayer a fortune. How many have been reprimanded or taken to court or have you tried to get money back from?

Sir Brian Bender: We have been trying to take money back from a number of valuers. I cannot remember the exact number but we have outstanding actions in terms of recompense from a number of valuers who we think were overpaid. I cannot immediately find that.

Q54 Mr Steinberg: You can write to me on that.

Sir Brian Bender: Nine valuer firms with the total sums involved being £1.2 million and a further 22 valuers claimed £223,000 over and above their entitlement. I can provide you with a note setting that out.[3]

Q55 Mr Steinberg: Who were they?

Sir Brian Bender: Again, I can provide that. I do not have that information.[4]

Q56 Mr Steinberg: Would you agree with me that the policy was wrong at the time and it was a recipe for the industry to sign blank cheques?

Sir Brian Bender: I would not put it in those words. As I said at the beginning of this hearing, in 2001 the fundamental policy decision at the time was nothing should get in the way of rapid slaughter. However, there are certainly lessons to be learned from last time about how we should have more effective controls in place, as I have just described.

Q57 Mr Steinberg: I want to move on quickly because I am trying to draw a picture here. I see the valuation as a major issue but, also, as I read this Report, as far as the taxpayer is concerned, I saw how much the cost of disinfecting the farm was costing and that was astronomical, absolutely astronomical. Turn to page 32, paragraph 4.14, please. "Current UK legislation allows the Department to require the farmer to meet the costs of cleansing and disinfection, but this provision was not used during the 2001 outbreak, to ensure a thorough and consistent approach was taken. In 2001 the Department spent around £300 million cleaning and disinfecting more than 10,000 premises—an average of £30,000 a farm." It goes on to say: "However, in the Netherlands, the average cost of initial disinfection was between £70 and £550 . . ." a farm. Let us say they were getting it done for nothing, and that was grossly cheap, it is a hell of a difference between £750 or £550 and £30,000. The point I am trying to make here is what with the valuers ripping everybody off, the people who were disinfecting ripping everybody off, the farmers were better off catching Foot and Mouth, were they not?

Sir Brian Bender: The fundamental difference between what we did in 2001 and what the Dutch did is that the Dutch made the farmers pay for the secondary cleansing and disinfection and we did not. Whether or not ministers will decide that we should change that policy in the future will be part of the overall consultation on the animal disease levy.

Q58 Mr Steinberg: Looking at this, quite honestly if I had been a farmer and I was struggling and I saw what was happening, I would have been tempted to put Foot and Mouth into the farm. You were going to make a fortune. It was the farmers who did not catch Foot and Mouth who were the ones who missed out. The ones who had it got an absolute fortune off the British taxpayer, that cannot be right. It was encouraging them, there was no deterrent.

Sir Brian Bender: The work we are doing on biosecurity, the tighter controls we have in place and the consultation we will be going out on later this year on a disease levy are intended to get those incentives in a better balance.

Q59 Mr Steinberg: If there was a future Foot and Mouth epidemic which, God forbid, will never be as bad as this again, are you saying the policy now will be to ensure that the compensation which will be given will be much better and clearly looked at and the disinfecting of the farms will be left to the farmers themselves to do through an insurance policy or something like that?

Sir Brian Bender: The answer to your question is yes. As I outlined earlier, some of the controls we have in place on valuation will be much more effective. On cleansing and disinfection, we also have much more effective controls in place but the current policy is still that the taxpayer will pay and whether or not that should be passed to the farmer will be part of the consultation on the disease levy.

Q60 Mr Steinberg: My last question at this stage: is it not about time that the policy was moved in the direction of the farmer being more responsible for his own livestock and land than the taxpayer and that an insurance policy for farmers, even if it is through DEFRA—I do not know—should be looked at and they should not depend upon 100% basic payment and compensation from the taxpayer?

Sir Brian Bender: The answer to your question is yes, though the route we prefer to go down and will be consulting on, I hope later this year, is a levy based system with a pump priming shared between the industry and Government. That is still a route to answering your question positively.

Mr Jenkins: Sir Brian, I am sitting here thinking can you tell me another industry where the risk associated with polluting or accident is picked up by the taxpayer?

Mr Curry: The coal industry.

Chairman: Mr Curry says the coal industry.

Q61 Mr Jenkins: Yes, the coal industry is an excellent industry. We paid out £2.4 billion to half a million people who worked in the industry who had been injured personally by their exposure to the industry. I do not think we could look at this as a one-off payment, this is a recurring situation, not only BSE but Foot and Mouth.

Sir Brian Bender: If you remember, it was just over a year ago when this Committee had a hearing on plant health—There are some areas where we have a legal requirement to compensate but, nonetheless, the question is the extent to which the farmer, animal keeper themselves should share that responsibility, and that is, as I said to Mr Steinberg, a direction we wish to move in.

Q62 Mr Jenkins: One of the things which amazes me, is on page 36 under figure 11, are examples of problems found on invoices submitted. Five down it says "Shredding of support documentation". Why do you think people shred documentation while there is a claim still proceeding?

Sir Brian Bender: Perhaps I can ask my Procurement Director, Mr Rabey?

Q63 Mr Jenkins: Did he shred the documentation?

Sir Brian Bender: No, but he is the one who has been pursuing these claims vigilantly since 2001.

Mr Rabey: The example of shredding documentation is currently with the police.

Q64 Mr Jenkins: Yes, it is fraud, is it not?

Sir Brian Bender: That is why it is with the police.

Q65 Mr Jenkins: There is a complete list of problems like that on the form which is an indication of the mindset of people involved in the industry.

Sir Brian Bender: Some of these were contractors that we are talking about who were not in the farming industry, but in the logistics part of it. We have been pursuing—in response to the Chairman's question earlier—cases where we think we have been overcharged very strongly for the last two or three years and in some cases through the courts. Where we can settle by mediation we are doing so.

Q66 Mr Jenkins: When Mr Steinberg pointed out to you some of the criticisms of the European Commission and particularly the cost—I loved your reasoning there, I thought that was bloody ingenious—this bull was a yearling bull and it is four months older and its valuation goes from £14,000 to £40,000, can you talk me through that, why they go up like that? If I had a bull I was selling worth £40,000 in four months' time, I do not think I would sell it for £14,000.

Sir Brian Bender: The information I have, as I say, is that the bull was a yearling, it was due to lay down a bank of semen for use in a champion herd. We did nonetheless query the valuation before paying it and the valuer said he had done it very thoroughly, it took two days and this would be an animal which was impossible to replace. Now that is one particular case so that is the information I have on that case.

Q67 Mr Jenkins: That was it. The valuer said it took two days to value this bull, the person who sold the bull four months ago did not realise the bull would be worth that much money and sold it for £14,000?
Sir Brian Bender: I think looking forward, the arrangements we have with the national list of valuers—which were described to Mr Steinberg—are intended to ensure, whatever happened in the past, there are not abuses in the future.

Q68 Mr Jenkins: We will look forward, we shall not look back because it is better to look forward with your Department rather than backwards. We are always promised one thing: things are going to get better. Then you come before this Committee and we are given promises. We are promised that the biosecurity and movement of animals in this country is far, far better than it has ever been and yet our Report shows there are offences still being committed today by farmers and animal movement people. What are you going to do to stop this?
Sir Brian Bender: Do you want to say what we are doing on the farm health plans clamping down on biosecurity?
Dr Reynolds: Yes. Farm health plans is one of the major initiatives in the animal health and welfare strategy and we have a working group there to look at sharing best practice. It is based on individual sectors. The pig sector is particularly active there. This is an area where each farm is going to be encouraged to have their own farm health plan to set out their approach individually to handle new risk. On biosecurity, it is one of the main considerations on bringing in the current animal movement regime which has to be associated with high standards of biosecurity. Only this week there is a new promotion on a poster and advertising campaign to particularly address biosecurity in markets.

Q69 Mr Jenkins: We can all sleep at night then, can we?
Dr Reynolds: It is all a question of reducing risk, is it not?

Q70 Mr Jenkins: What are you going to do to stop it? There are people out there who are not complying with the rules and regulations, what are you doing to stop it?
Sir Brian Bender: Through targeted inspections co-ordinated between local government and the State Veterinary Service based on risk assessments.

Q71 Mr Jenkins: Are we setting up those targeted inspections? What plan have you got and what risk analysis have you done? What wagons are you stopping because it is a high risk index?
Ms Stacey: We have a framework agreement in place with local authorities which enables local authorities to work with our SVS staff to identify on a risk-based approach those which they should be targeting. That is done taking into account the

nature and scale of the businesses that we are looking at and also it allows for local knowledge to be put in.

Q72 Mr Jenkins: Excellent. Where is the highest risk area? Is it a particular geographical area or is it a particular commodity?
Dr Reynolds: There are a number of areas of risk. The particular risks are in areas of high animal density and where there are significant movements of animals.

Q73 Mr Jenkins: Yes.
Dr Reynolds: Those are two particular risk areas and that is why, of course, the animal movement regime was brought in with a six day standstill from the time of arrival of a consignment of animals on a farm before further animals could move off: six days in the case of cattle and sheep and 20 days for pigs.

Q74 Mr Jenkins: You are satisfied that your inspection regime is rigid enough to stop and reduce the number of infringements we are seeing today in the industry?
Sir Brian Bender: No. I am satisfied with the second verb you used, "reduce". There is more we have to do in terms of risk based targeted inspection to deal with these.

Q75 Mr Jenkins: Tell me what you have to do?
Sir Brian Bender: We have to pursue more the sort of approach that Ms Stacey was referring to a few minutes ago.
Ms Stacey: That is right. We do have operational partners out there: local authorities, trading standards officers, for example. We have a pool of local knowledge but we need to be more systematic in exchanging that and making decisions about what to do with it.

Q76 Mr Jenkins: I think I have seen a figure in the Report that 23% of vehicles stopped either did not have the correct documentation or the vehicle itself was not acceptable. What sort of figure would you like to see, 10%, 5%? What is your target percentage of movements that the police or authorities would stop that would meet the laid down criteria?
Ms Stacey: The approach has been to identify those sites that are highest risk, for example every vehicle that is moving in and out of the market is actually checked. The approach has been to identify high risk.

Q77 Mr Jenkins: 23% at the present time, so what is the figure that you are targeting? Is it 10%, 20%? When do you intend to meet the target?
Sir Brian Bender: I cannot answer that. We can provide a note if it would help.[5]

---

[5] Ev 22

Q78 Mr Jenkins: I have not even got off page one yet. If there was another outbreak, how confident are you that you would get that outbreak notified within two days of it being identified or being picked up?

Sir Brian Bender: How confident is a very difficult question to answer. Through the combination of greater awareness, through the information we have put out to farmers, through the increased emphasis on biosecurity, through our own surveillance strategy that the Chief Vet can say more about, through the inspection arrangements, we would be more optimistic than we were. Will there ever be another Bobby Waugh, I cannot say that. We are talking about risk reduction here.

Q79 Mr Jenkins: Does your contingency plan take into consideration the deliberate introduction of the disease on our farms?

Sir Brian Bender: Yes. First of all, at a general level it is hard to imagine a deliberate introduction of one strain being more damaging than it was in 2001 when there was a virus on over 50 farms in a very geographically dispersed area. Our contingency plan is intended to deal with that sort of situation. Secondly, if there were a number of different strains, which deliberate introduction could involve, we believe that the combination of diagnosis, laboratory facilities and, indeed, if it came to it, vaccination antigens could also tackle that. Certainly our planning addresses the possibility of deliberate introduction either of a single strain, which as I say would be the same sort of situation, or of several strains.

Q80 Mr Jenkins: I have got one last question. Your IT system, the ExDS system, has been delayed. Is this system not needed or not necessary? If it is needed and necessary, why has it not been given a higher priority?

Sir Brian Bender: It will be necessary. It will be an improvement. The reason it was delayed was essentially because when we looked at the issue with IBM, our new partners, they thought it was better to press the pause button rather than grind on and have what this Committee would certainly recognise as an IT systems failure. We are significantly better off now than we were at the beginning of the 2001 outbreak because the system we have now is the one that was operating effectively by the end of the outbreak and has been improved since then. We have an adequate IT system but it is not as good as we would like.

Q81 Mr Jenkins: Can I ask was this system stopped at the Gateway process?

Sir Brian Bender: I do not think it was a Gateway, as it happens, I think it was a fresh look taken at it because we had a new partnership with IBM that DEFRA has entered into.

Mr Jenkins: My time is up, unfortunately.

Chairman: Thank you very much. Mr Davidson.

Q82 Mr Davidson: I wonder if I can just follow on the point about animal tracking, in particular looking at paragraph 2.10 where it mentions the exercise undertaken in March 2004. As I read that, 23% of the vehicles stopped were breaking the law. Can I ask what actions were taken?

Sir Brian Bender: I do not know whether any of my colleagues can answer that. If not, I am sorry, we will have to provide you with a note on that.[6]

Q83 Mr Davidson: That gives us an indication of how seriously this is taken. How many actions like this, exercises like this, have there been since?

Sir Brian Bender: Again, I am sorry, we are not able to answer that question.

Q84 Mr Davidson: Nobody can tell me that. That does not give me an indication of how seriously you take this. A major exercise, as I read it here, with 43 police forces involved found 23% of vehicles stopped were breaking the law, and you cannot tell me whether or not you have had another exercise like that since or are planning one.

Sir Brian Bender: I can say that we are planning one for later this year. What I cannot say is how many others there have been.[7]

Q85 Mr Davidson: Goodness me. I think you will understand why we have always thought that your Department is somewhat complacent. You cannot tell me whether or not any actions were taken, you cannot tell me whether or not there have been any other exercises. Can I turn to paragraph 2.9 where I see that there were 73,000-odd inspections. Mention is made here of 182 prosecutions. Can I ask whether or not there were any cases where advice or anything similar was taken short of prosecution? Is it prosecution or nothing in these circumstances, or can you not tell me that?

Sir Brian Bender: I am sure there are cases where there was advice. I am just looking at whether prosecutions resulted in convictions. There were 182 prosecutions in 2003 and 38 convictions.

Q86 Mr Davidson: I am going to come to that in a minute. What I was asking you was whether or not there were actions taken short of prosecution and, if so, how many of them were there?

Sir Brian Bender: I believe the answer is yes, but I am afraid I cannot answer that question specifically.[8]

Q87 Mr Davidson: That is a do not know, right. How many of the prosecutions initiated are still under way or have they all been completed and there were only 38 convictions?

Sir Brian Bender: Not all of them have yet come to a conclusion. I have a figure in front of me that talks about 350 in total initiated, 99 convictions so far. There were 182 prosecutions in 2003 and 38 convictions out of that lot. As I say, not all of the numbers have yet come to a conclusion.

Q88 Mr Davidson: Maybe you can give us a note on that. These figures are somewhat confusing, I suspect they are on a different time basis. Can I ask in terms of penalties, for the prosecutions that were successful what level of penalty was that, or can you not tell me that?
Sir Brian Bender: Again, I am sorry. I think rather than waste your time now we will cover that in a note.[9]

Q89 Mr Davidson: Can you name the people who were involved?
Sir Brian Bender: The punishments are generally fines. There was one that was a two month prison sentence.

Q90 Mr Davidson: How big were the fines?
Sir Brian Bender: I do not have that figure, I am sorry.

Q91 Mr Davidson: Okay. Do you have any idea whether or not the punishment is likely to be a deterrent?
Sir Brian Bender: In the case of a two month prison term for one cattle movement, that would certainly appear to be a deterrent.

Q92 Mr Davidson: That would seem to be the case. It depends how much the gain was. If you had a one in 10 million chance of being caught and going to jail for two months and the gain was £1 million, that is an acceptable risk/reward ratio. I am just seeking clarification on this but you cannot give me any.
Sir Brian Bender: I have not come prepared, and I apologise for that.[10]

Q93 Mr Davidson: Can I turn to the question of vaccination. On page 22, paragraph 3.14, I think the text here sums this up pretty well: "The Department decided against the use of vaccination—mainly due to resistance from farmers who feared that vaccination would be economically damaging". I think we took the view at the time that the Department was too weak to stand up to farmers. Is that still the case?
Sir Brian Bender: There were two reasons at the time why vaccination did not happen. One was as stated there, the other was an assurance being sought from the supermarkets that they would sell vaccinated product. The two come back to the same point. Looking forward, as I said in reply to an earlier question, vaccination to live would be at the forefront of our disease control policies and we have been discussing that and the acceptability of it with the whole food chain.

Q94 Mr Davidson: Let me just get this clear. The two arguments against vaccination were both concerned with the farmers putting their own profits ahead of the cost to the taxpayer of allowing the Foot and Mouth epidemic to spread. They were vetoing the use of vaccination because it might cost them money because the cost to the taxpayer was effectively a nil

cost to them, so in a sense it was entirely rational, though selfish, for farmers to say, "We do not wish to vaccinate" because they might lose money out of it. That is a correct summation, is it not?
Sir Brian Bender: It was not axiomatic in 2001 that vaccination would bring the disease under control more quickly, that was one of the issues at the time.

Q95 Mr Davidson: There was a point though when you thought it would and you wanted to do that but the farmers stopped you doing that.
Sir Brian Bender: There was a point in, I think, late March, early April 2001 when the then Chief Vet recommended vaccination of cattle in one or maybe two areas under certain conditions, and farmer acceptability, because otherwise they could not get the needles in, was one of the conditions.

Q96 Mr Davidson: The vets recommended that and because the farmers would not allow it you did not do it. That is correct, is it not?
Sir Brian Bender: The policy decision by ministers at the time was that conditions were not right for the reasons I stated earlier.

Q97 Mr Davidson: Because farmers would not accept it.
Sir Brian Bender: Because of objections by farmers to the loss of economic value and the supermarkets.

Q98 Mr Davidson: We are still in exactly the same position really.
Sir Brian Bender: I do not believe we are. I think as a result of the discussions we have been having since then with the food chain and what we have said publicly in our contingency plan, vaccination to live will be at the forefront. It may not be right in a particular set of circumstances.

Q99 Mr Davidson: If you look half way down paragraph 3.15 after the first blue dot, about seven lines down, there is a section there, I think in the third sentence, where it says: "Some farmers might therefore oppose vaccination and prefer their livestock to be culled." That is really saying that farmers would prefer to kill their animals rather than have them vaccinated and allow them to live because it is more profitable to them to have their animals killed, is it not? That is really what that is saying.
Sir Brian Bender: That is saying what some farmers might, therefore, feel.

Q100 Mr Davidson: Indeed. In the circumstances that some farmers continue to feel that, would you be overruling them and proceeding with vaccination despite the objections of farmers or would farmers have a veto again with the bill falling on the taxpayer?
Sir Brian Bender: I would very much hope—

Q101 Mr Davidson: I am not saying "hope".
Sir Brian Bender: It is Government policy that in the right circumstances vaccination to live would be a disease control.

Q102 Mr Davidson: I understand that. These are not the questions I am asking you. I understand why you are trying to avoid answering them. In circumstances where vets recommend vaccination and farmers say that they wish not to have their animals vaccinated, would you have the power and the authority to proceed with vaccination?

Dr Reynolds: We would have a Statutory Instrument to vaccinate in a vaccination zone.

Sir Brian Bender: We would have the legal power to do it.

Q103 Mr Davidson: Against the objections of farmers?

Sir Brian Bender: Legally, yes, the question is one of policy.

Q104 Mr Davidson: I understand that.

Sir Brian Bender: We will have the legal power.

Q105 Mr Davidson: I understand that. I just want to be absolutely clear. Can I come back to paragraph 4.14 to this question of disinfecting. I am in a state of some confusion here because what I cannot quite understand is why the Department pays for the cleaning up of farmers' buildings and farms when they are effectively private businesses. I can think of no other circumstances where this is done at state expense. Is there any parallel that you can think of?

Sir Brian Bender: I cannot think of a parallel. The reason—

Q106 Mr Davidson: I understand the reason.

Sir Brian Bender: The reason is to ensure the disease does not recrudesce, which it did in 1997.

Q107 Mr Davidson: That is the reason why you want them cleaned. What I was asking was why the state pays for that and not farmers. Can you clarify that for me?

Sir Brian Bender: The answer is that is a policy ministers wish to review in the context of animal disease.

Q108 Mr Davidson: The point you used in your defence was that you were having them cleaned to make sure they were cleaned properly and the disease did not proceed on the basis that farmers could not be trusted to do it themselves, yet in a substantial number of cases the farmers were contracted by the Department to do it. Am I the only person here who thinks that is somewhat anomalous, that if they cannot be trusted to do it on their own you pay them and then trust them to do it when you are paying them?

Sir Brian Bender: The issue is the supervision of the work, which we—

Q109 Mr Davidson: They can be supervised by themselves when they are being paid for it by you.

Sir Brian Bender: For the future we will have supervision of all disinfection work in a more effective way than we had in 2001.

Q110 Mr Davidson: I certainly hope so. I wonder if I could just finally turn to the question of this table 10 on page 36. The first one, File No 2, compensation of a quarter of a million paid for animals not in fact slaughtered, that is fraud, is it not?

Sir Brian Bender: The money in question has been recovered.

Q111 Mr Davidson: I did not ask you that. I said is that fraud? Yes or no? Is it fraud?

Sir Brian Bender: I do not know is the answer because I think it depends on the circumstances.

Q112 Mr Davidson: If you do not know, that is fair enough.

Sir Brian Bender: I do not know because if one is dealing with farmers in this sort of stressful situation, did they knowingly send valuations of animals that were not killed?

Q113 Mr Davidson: A quarter of a million pounds, you do not submit an expenses claim for a quarter of a million pounds unknowingly.

Sir Brian Bender: The payment has been recovered, £240,000.

Q114 Mr Davidson: You do not know whether or not any prosecution or any action has followed?

Sir Brian Bender: I do not know. I do not think there has been any prosecution but I do not know.

Q115 Mr Davidson: Why would there not be a prosecution?

Sir Brian Bender: I will look into that.[11]

Q116 Mr Davidson: I would certainly hope so. Moving on to File No.7, the one beneath that, is that not also fraud as well where the cattle described was as "mostly pedigree bred from top sires", I think there were 317 of them, and they were only able to produce certificates for nine. Unless that is carelessness and the certificates had been lost, surely like the MOT you can get a duplicate. That would be fraud as well, would it not?

Sir Brian Bender: The issue here was whether the documentation was available subsequently for the Commission and, as I think the Report says, farmers were not under a legal obligation to maintain the documentation. The issue for the future is the extent to which we will have controls in place at the time rather than retrospectively.

Q117 Mr Davidson: Why should a farmer not keep the certification?

Sir Brian Bender: We are talking about a year or two later when the Commission came round.

Q118 Mr Davidson: The final one I want to ask you about in terms of fraud is File No 59. Do you think somebody made a mistake claiming milk production of 10,000 litres a year when, in fact, it was just above the average of 6,500? That seems like fraud to me as well actually. How did that get past your system? This is the Commission picking these things up. I think we have adversely commented in the past on the European Commission's lax attitude towards spending but here we find that lax though they might be they are tighter than yours. Is this fraud, do you think?

Sir Brian Bender: I do not know whether it is fraud but what I do know is that controls we now have in place for a future outbreak would ensure much more effective oversight of these issues.

Q119 Mr Davidson: Last time you gave us all sorts of assurances that the systems you had in place were adequate.

Sir Brian Bender: That was in relation to lessons we have learned from 2001. We are still looking back at the 2001 outbreak.

Q120 Chairman: Just to get it right, for the future your present plan is to do a mass vaccination around the outbreak because you think you have now squared the farmers and the supermarkets?

Sir Brian Bender: Not necessarily, Chairman. Our plan with any outbreak—

Q121 Chairman: Sir Brian, I know you have got a right to answer the question but I think it is terribly important that we get this right because there was a feeling in the last outbreak that there was a lot of uncertainty within Government and there was a huge debate going on about vaccination. I think it is very important that at this sort of hearing, calmly, before an outbreak takes place, we know exactly what is going to happen in the future.

Sir Brian Bender: Let me try and if I get anything slightly wrong I will ask the Chief Vet to supplement it. The EU law requires slaughter of susceptible animals on infected premises and dangerous contacts, so if farmer A has gone to farm B or the animals have moved. That will happen anyway in any outbreak.

Q122 Chairman: Everybody accepts that, that is the traditional way of doing it. You cull all the animals on the farm and on the neighbouring farms.

Sir Brian Bender: Not necessarily.

Q123 Chairman: It was completely different in the last outbreak. You were culling animals at farms three kilometres away and there were mass pyres. The public now want a clear statement about what is going to happen in the future.

Sir Brian Bender: Last time round we supplemented that policy part way through, the policy I have just described, by a contiguous cull which involved all neighbouring farms. There is a distinction self-evidently between dangerous contacts, which of course, will include some neighbouring farms, and all neighbouring farms. The first line of disease control will be slaughter of susceptible animals on infected premises and dangerous contacts. We then

have, and the NAO Report contains it, this decision tree about what we do next. I cannot sit before this Committee and say there will never be another contiguous cull; what I can say, as we have made clear in the contingency plan, is emergency vaccination to live will be considered as a disease control option from the start of any Foot and Mouth outbreak.

Q124 Chairman: Can I ask the expert. We have got the benefit of the Chief Veterinary Officer here, a distinguished lady with a lifetime of experience. What is your view? Here you are at a Parliamentary Committee, if there is another outbreak, we all accept that on farms where there is direct contact you kill the animals, that has always happened, but what we had in the last outbreak was completely different with this contiguous cull. There were many, many animals being slaughtered and subsequently we found no disease on those farms whatsoever. You are the Chief Veterinary Officer, from your experience will you now tell the Committee that you will try and get in a system which relies on vaccination so that we can stop this mass culling of animals?

Dr Reynolds: Yes, I will tell the Committee that. The culling of infected premises and dangerous contacts is the first policy but from day one we will be looking at emergency vaccination to allow the animals to go on and live. That has been made clear. The decision tree makes it obvious that there are a number of practical situations which will need to be considered in any outbreak. Those include the strain of virus during the epidemic and whether there is a vaccine in the bank that can be made up. It will also include the species of animals infected and the extent to which there may have been any silent or unapparent infection at an early stage. Those are the considerations which will need to be put into an analysis of any decision to vaccinate. The practical arrangements can be implemented five days after confirmation of disease provided the vaccine is present in the bank.

Q125 Mr Steinberg: Can I ask a question? I am totally baffled. Why do they not vaccinate animals now?

Dr Reynolds: The national herd and flocks may be vaccinated against particular problems, like leptospirosis and so on, but there is no background vaccination for Foot and Mouth Disease. In fact, it is banned in Europe as a prophylactic measure.

Q126 Mr Steinberg: As a what?

Sir Brian Bender: If you vaccinate on a regular basis in order to avoid the animal catching the disease, that is prophylactic vaccination. That is not considered a cost-effective measure and it is not advised by the veterinary experts.

Dr Reynolds: Furthermore, if I can just add, it does mean that you have got a considerable ongoing cost of vaccination, so it is of very great advantage to be free from Foot and Mouth Disease.

DEFRA and NFU

Q127 Mr Steinberg: We do eat vaccinated meat now but vaccinated for other diseases, is that right?
Sir Brian Bender: Correct.

Q128 Mr Steinberg: So what is the difference between meat vaccinated for one disease against another disease?
Sir Brian Bender: None.

Q129 Mr Steinberg: What did you say? None? What the hell is all the trouble about?
Sir Brian Bender: People in Argentina have been eating meat vaccinated for Foot and Mouth for many years, so there is no public health issue here and the Food Standards Agency are on the record as saying that.

Q130 Mr Davidson: Farmers are still against it.
Sir Brian Bender: Not necessarily. Mr Davidson says that farmers are still against it but I do not believe the farming industry is against it. The NAO Report has a sentence talking about "some farmers may take this view". Some farmers would be against it but I do not believe the NFU, as the leadership of the farming industry, is against the use of vaccination in the future, not from the conversations we have had with them.

Q131 Mr Davidson: So they have moved from their previous position?
Sir Brian Bender: That is my understanding, yes.
Mr Davidson: That is helpful.

Q132 Chairman: I do not really like these words, "my understanding". This is a vitally important issue, surely you can give a clearer indication than that.
Sir Brian Bender: I will confirm this in writing formally to the Committee afterwards having double-checked with the National Farmers' Union, but I believe that the National Farmers' Union have moved since the 2001 outbreak as a result of the discussions since then and the discussions we have had and the discussions they have had publicly.[12]

Q133 Chairman: What does the Chief Veterinary Officer say about this? She must know this matter intimately, she must know exactly what is going on in discussions with the NFU.
Dr Reynolds: I have not got anything to add to the comments of the Permanent Secretary because the meetings that have been held with stakeholders on this have reached that view.

Q134 Chairman: They are now happy with vaccination, are they?
Dr Reynolds: The issues around vaccination are about whether or not it is going to be effective in helping the control of the disease and the practical considerations I have pointed out, whether or not vaccine is available and whether or not the practical

situation is going to show benefits. The practical preparations are in place for that to be launched as the vaccination to live policy.
Mr Curry: Chairman, as the Parliamentary Officer for the NFU is in the audience, if he was spontaneously to provoke his vice president to write to tell us, would it not be much easier than trying to get it through a third party?

Q135 Chairman: Where is he? Do you want to say anything?
Mr Holbeche: I am sure we could write a letter to you, Chairman, which would confirm what the Permanent Secretary has said.[13]

Q136 Chairman: Thank you very much.
Sir Brian Bender: Can I also say, Chairman, that in the exercise that we carried out last summer that is referred to in the Report and goes under the name of Exercise Hornbeam, the policy decision was made to vaccinate to live in certain regions of the country. So Ministers and civil servants, having played this war game, as Mr Curry put it, took a decision to vaccinate in that exercise last summer.

Q137 Mr Steinberg: If they vaccinated and let the animals live but we would still not eat the meat, would that have been more expensive than the cull that took place and the compensation? Do you understand what I mean?
Sir Brian Bender: I understand the question. I do not know what the position was in 2001. By the time we were at the crucial stage of whether or not to vaccinate, the number of cases per day had already peaked, or was about to peak, but I do not know whether overall it would have been more cost-effective or not.

Q138 Chairman: If you could let us have a note about that we would be very grateful.
Sir Brian Bender: I am sorry, can I just say our cost-benefit analysis work should help answer these questions.[14]

Q139 Mrs Browning: Chairman, could I just ask Dr Reynolds a couple of questions based on what I was asking Sir Brian earlier. Dr Reynolds, I am wondering if you were aware that Bobby Waugh was contravening Article 21(2) of the Animal Byproducts Order 1999.
Dr Reynolds: What I am aware of in connection with Bobby Waugh is that was the origin of Foot and Mouth Disease, it was the index case, and that the feeding of unprocessed swill was considered to be the main contribution.

Q140 Mrs Browning: Are you familiar with Article 21(2) of your own Department's regulations? Can I quote it for you? It does not talk about feeding, it says: "No person shall bring unprocessed catering waste on to any premises where pigs are kept". I am asking again, are you aware that he was

---

contravening that Order? Not what he fed his pigs but the fact that he brought on to his premises unprocessed catering waste, are you aware of that?
Sir Brian Bender: We are.

Q141 Mrs Browning: I am sorry, I am really asking Dr Reynolds. I am asking if you are aware of it, Dr Reynolds. You are either aware of it or you are not, I do not think it requires a long answer.
Sir Brian Bender: Are you asking at the time or are you asking—

Q142 Mrs Browning: I am asking if you are aware now. No, I am sorry, I am asking Dr Reynolds. Do not worry, you will get your turn. I am sorry, it is a very straightforward question. You are either aware, Dr Reynolds, or you are not.
Dr Reynolds: I am aware that there was thought to be unprocessed catering waste on the forecourt of Bobby Waugh's premises. Whether or not it was being fed is something that I do not know.

Q143 Mrs Browning: You do not know whether it was being fed but you are aware that he was in contravention of your own Animal Byproducts Order 1999, Article 21(2), which specifically says: "No person shall bring unprocessed catering waste on to any premises where pigs are kept".
Dr Reynolds: I am aware that he was prosecuted for several offences, including under the Animal Byproducts Order.

Q144 Mrs Browning: Okay. Can I ask you then are you aware now that Mr Jim Dring made his signed submission to the Anderson Inquiry in which he admitted he was aware that Bobby Waugh was bringing unprocessed catering waste on to Burnside Farm in contravention of that same Order?
Dr Reynolds: I am aware, as the Permanent Secretary said earlier, that there was a personal statement which was not submitted to the Anderson Inquiry.

Q145 Mrs Browning: You are aware from what Mr Dring said in that submission, whether it went to the Anderson Inquiry or not, he admits—one of your officers—that he was aware that there was contravention of that Order at the time he had responsibility for that farm.
Dr Reynolds: As I understand it, this is a question about whether or not the forecourt of this farm was part of the premises or not and it seems that might be an area that we can write and give further details on.[15]

Q146 Mrs Browning: I have got a map here of the farm. It is your own departmental map. I am looking at what it says here as "Waste Delivery Point". It looks pretty much to me as though it is part of the farm. This is the DEFRA map that was used as evidence in the court case. I am happy to give you the map if you want to refresh your memory.[16]

Sir Brian Bender: Clearly we are not satisfying you with our replies as to what our current state of knowledge is. I do undertake that we will write setting out very clearly what the position is.

Q147 Mrs Browning: I appreciate that and you have already promised to write to us, but I just want to test the current awareness of the Chief Veterinary Officer now that we have been through all of these inquiries and you are appearing before us for the second time. I now want to test what your awareness is of what has been done by your own officials.
Dr Reynolds: I am aware that there was a personal statement that was made by Jim Dring and that was not submitted to the Anderson Inquiry. It deals with what he considered might have been the situation with the benefit of hindsight and that is about the nature of the Waugh farm, which was originally licensed for processing but was not thought to be processing at the time.

Q148 Mrs Browning: It is not a matter of processing. I am sorry to have to come back to this, Chairman, but it is actually about understanding your own regulations which the State Veterinary Office have to apply when they apply the law. I have got a copy of the Orders here. If I can just quote it to you. Article 21(2) of the Animal Byproducts Order 1999 states: "No person shall bring unprocessed catering waste on to any premises where pigs are kept". The reason I am asking this, apart from testing your own awareness of what the situation is now with all these various statements, is the fact that no licence should have ever been given to somebody who was contravening one of your own regulations, should it?
Sir Brian Bender: If they were contravened. Would you allow Ms Stacey to respond particularly on the question of the geography of the farm because of the three of us she has actually seen a photograph of it from above.
Ms Stacey: I have not seen the large scale map that you have there but I have seen a photograph of the hard standing in front of the farm at Burnside. The photograph shows the flat concrete hard standing and behind that the gate to the farm. That hard standing was not regarded as part and parcel of the farm by our veterinary inspectors and, indeed, was not seen to be within the general curtilage of the farm. Our understanding is it was used on occasions for material to be dropped off there on its way to another farm just a few hundred yards down the same road which actually was involved in the processing of swill and that was a local arrangement between the two farmers, but it was not regarded by us as within the curtilage of the farm when doing inspections.

Q149 Mrs Browning: You are saying that was outside the curtilage of the farm?
Ms Stacey: It was regarded as such, yes.

Q150 Mrs Browning: I have to say that anybody looking at this map and seeing its proximity to shed four and shed five I do not think would agree with that. I would like a more detailed response when you respond to me. Sir Brian, when you do reply, just for clarity, I would like your consideration that if Mr Dring had carried out the enforcement of the regulations as I believe he should have done that we would not perhaps have seen Foot and Mouth at Burnside Farm at all because he would not have been licensed.

Sir Brian Bender: I will cover that in the further note I provide to the Committee.

Q151 Mrs Browning: Finally, and this is my last question, could you tell me who you think is responsible, whether you think it is Mr Waugh and what he carried out in contravention of the legislation there, or whether you think it was down to the enforcement agencies that should have checked it?

Sir Brian Bender: Mrs Beckett was asked this question of who is to blame, I think, before the EFRA Select Committee—whether it was when Mr Curry or Mr Jack was chairing it—and her answer was: "The person who brought the meat illegally into the country in the first place, point one. Point two, the farmer who did not report it". However, I would not for a moment pretend that the enforcement authorities, including my own Department, do not have a responsibility for effective inspection enforcement to deal with these situations. So, yes, we have a responsibility.

Q152 Mrs Browning: Finally, in terms of the map, when you respond on that particular point, is it clear in your understanding, because we know that unprocessed waste food was stored on the premises, not just fed but stored, whether you know where the storage took place, not just where it was received in terms of the waste delivery point which is clearly identified? Where on the premises was the food stored, or maybe you do not know.

Ms Stacey: The position is that we were aware that food was stored on the hard standing, it was never seen inside the premises.

Q153 Mrs Browning: Stored or taken delivery of?

Ms Stacey: It was stored on the hard standing. It was not destined for this particular farm, it was on its way to be processed at a farm further down the road. It was never seen as stored on Burnside Farm. At the same time, my understanding is that when Jim Dring was there to inspect, he was inspecting a farm that was feeding and had a licence to feed processed swill. He did not see unprocessed swill being fed to pigs on that farm. He did a job of inspecting the arrangements for processed swill feed.

Mrs Browning: Thank you.

Q154 Mr Curry: Could we just be clear. If in the course of an outbreak it came to the decision whether or not to use vaccination, that decision would be taken by ministers, would it?

Sir Brian Bender: Yes, on the advice of—

Q155 Mr Curry: I accept that.

Sir Brian Bender: The answer to the question is yes.

Q156 Mr Curry: There would not be a delegated responsibility to use vaccination.

Sir Brian Bender: It would not be delegated. There is a presumption that—

Q157 Mr Curry: Ministers obviously get advice but it would be a ministerial decision.

Sir Brian Bender: Correct.

Q158 Mr Curry: Can we also be clear that nobody is talking about universal preventative vaccination?

Sir Brian Bender: Correct.

Q159 Mr Curry: Can we also be clear that nobody is talking about trying to vaccinate sheep because they have got to be gathered together and if you think you have vaccinated them and one has not been vaccinated you are worse than if you had not started, is that right?

Sir Brian Bender: I am not sure about the rationale that you describe but the answer is you are correct, it is not part of our plan to vaccinate sheep.

Q160 Mr Curry: Finally, a question for the Chief Vet. There have been suggestions that live Foot and Mouth Disease can run through sheep herds and out again the other side without our being aware. What do we know about that?

Dr Reynolds: Certainly in 2001 there was a particularly prevalent mild strain of Foot and Mouth Disease which was not easy to detect. It was detectable but not easy.

Q161 Mr Curry: If one detected that sort of strain what would one do, let it run its course?

Dr Reynolds: No, not at all. This is a notifiable disease so there is a policy, which has already been described, of removing the infected premises and the dangerous contacts and it would apply equally to a mild strain as to one of the very virulent strains.

Q162 Mr Curry: It is also much more difficult in sheep if they are spread out over the fells, as we know for the purposes of claims.

Sir Brian Bender: That was one of the issues in 2001 when the animals were up on the fells. The issue was not what happened when they were up there because it could not spread any further, the issue was what would happen when they came down and when it would then spread.

Q163 Mr Curry: Have we now got an adequate record of digital maps of where agricultural holdings are? The reason I ask is in my constituency DEFRA seemed to have this view of farms all being in one place with a hedge around them and an entrance and an exit and a farmhouse, it was all slightly like *Alice in Wonderland* or Marie Antoinette, and yet in my constituency you can have a holding spread over seven or eight separate locations. There was a problem there. Some farms turned out to be spread all the way offshore. Are we sure we know where they all are?

Sir Brian Bender: I am very conscious from previous hearings of this Committee about the issue of farms being identified as in the sea. The land register that we have is being used this year by the Rural Payments Agency for the Single Farm Payment. There has been a process of confirmation and ratification by farmers, of which there is a backlog, but very significant progress has been made on that.

Q164 Mr Curry: Could I just come back to the vets for a minute. We talked about contingency plans in terms of the overall structures but what plans are there to mobilise vets from beyond the State Veterinary Service, because it is obviously a fairly tight service and you would need to deploy people from outside? What are the contingency plans there?

Ms Stacey: That is right. We have got about 290 vets employed in the Service at the moment and about six temporary veterinary inspectors as well, so our numbers are up on what they were in 2001. We have got them freed up now from the management tasks that were burdensome in 2001, so there is more resource there actually applied in the field. We have also got arrangements in place to use vets from the Veterinary Laboratories Agency and we have got some 19 centres around England that we can tap into. As you know, we work with some 7,000 private veterinarians and we would call upon them, as we have done in the past. Currently, we are piloting arrangements to develop a cadre of private vets trained in specific emergency response roles. That is going on at the moment in four of our offices.

Q165 Mr Curry: There has been an analogy with the Territorial Army.

Ms Stacey: Yes, that is right. The pilot is going very well, it should finish in June and I am very hopeful there will be a good outcome there. We would then extend that to all 24 offices so we will end up with at least another 100 private vets specifically trained to take on roles in an emergency. Looking further afield, we have the international reserve arrangements where we can call on government vets from other countries, for example from Australia, New Zealand, Canada, USA. I think we are much better placed.

Q166 Mr Curry: We have talked about the levy scheme a little bit. When you were asked about that before, Sir Brian, you said that the debate has all been rather subsumed into a more general debate about charging and regulation on the industry. I think that was what you said. Can you tell me a little more about that?

Sir Brian Bender: I seem to remember in your previous incarnation as Chairman of the EFRA Select Committee, Mr Curry, you asked more than once does the Department believe the polluter should pay, and actually in this sector more generally it is a rule that is not systematically applied. What we are doing at the moment is looking at the cumulative impact of changes to the Common

Agricultural Policy, first of all, and what that will mean, the hopeful relaxation of the Over 30 Month Scheme and the different regulations in the pipeline and the application of a polluter pays system, to try to get an overview of the cumulative impact on the industry and, within that, the place of a cost sharing animal levy system.

Q167 Mr Curry: Why do you think a levy is preferable to an insurance scheme? Have you tested a model against an insurance scheme or talked to the industry about it?

Sir Brian Bender: In talking to both the insurance industry and the farming industry, it looks to be a more likely route forward in the short to medium-term. We have conducted some independent research on attitudes and intentions and this looks to be a more fruitful route forward for disease type situations. There are circumstances in other countries where farmers have insurance for other things but less so for disease, so in our environment this looks a more fruitful route forward.

Q168 Mr Curry: No doubt there will be a debate when this is eventually consulted on more widely. Finally, if I may, are you now confident that meat imports are as under control as they can be? We have had many happy hours of discussion about this at the airport, as you will recall.

Sir Brian Bender: Yes, and, as I understand it, the National Audit Office are doing a Report at the moment on Customs enforcement. I think the answer is we have reduced the risks through awareness raising and through the enforcement activities of Customs. The risk is significantly reduced. It will never be zero and no doubt the NAO Report that is coming forward in a couple of months' time will address this particular aspect.

Q169 Mr Curry: If I may have a very brief postscript. You are confident that farmers have restocked, but the interesting thing is that most people who got Foot and Mouth Disease did restock whereas reductions have been in the arable sector which had nothing to do with the Foot and Mouth crisis. You are confident that people have restocked with animals other than cattle which have been brought in with TB?

Sir Brian Bender: I am trying to work out your double negatives.

Q170 Mr Curry: Bovine TB is now the main cause of concern of animal disease.

Sir Brian Bender: It certainly is and it is also likely to be the case that some of the spread of TB outside a certain part of the country was as a result of movements when restocking happened.

Q171 Mr Curry: That is a debate which is ongoing.

Sir Brian Bender: Correct.

Q172 Mr Jenkins: On page 35, at 5.5, about a third of the way down it says: "The Commission examined a sample of 100 large compensation awards but found that the rationale for the valuation was largely absent from the files. Its enquiries with farmers and valuers produced explanations which the Commission found to be weak and unconvincing. Many of the farmers and valuers contacted by the Commission refused, or were unable, to provide documentary evidence to support claims . . ." In 2002 the Department assured this Committee that valuation of stock undertaken by professional valuers on behalf of the Department was well supported. Which is true?

Sir Brian Bender: We did as much work as we could on reconciliation but there is no doubt there were issues there and the Commission reported what they have reported.

Q173 Mr Jenkins: What you said to the Committee was based on what, some assurance?

Sir Brian Bender: That was based on the best reconciliation we were able to do. We had dozens of staff at each of the Disease Control Centres doing that reconciliation. It was not possible to do a perfect reconciliation and that is what the Commission pursued with us.

Q174 Mr Jenkins: So some evaluations were a little lie, a bit overvalued?

Sir Brian Bender: I repeat the point I have made a couple of times in this hearing about the relative overvaluation in Britain compared with other infected countries in 2001.

Q175 Mr Jenkins: We do not have the Chief Officers from the other countries in front of us at the moment. If these valuations were high, have we taken any action against the valuers to recover some of the money?

Sir Brian Bender: There have been one or two cases that I referred to earlier where we have been pursuing the valuers.

Q176 Mr Jenkins: With the new approved list of valuers, are any of the valuers that you have taken action against on the new approved list?

Sir Brian Bender: I hope the answer to that is no. I will ensure that the note I provide to the Committee, which I think I promised you earlier on this point, will address that question directly.[17]

Mr Jenkins: Thank you.

Q177 Mr Steinberg: Presumably you have been to New Zealand, Sir Brian?

Sir Brian Bender: Actually I have not, I wish I had.

Q178 Mr Steinberg: Really, that does surprise me.

Sir Brian Bender: My loss.

Q179 Mr Steinberg: Permanent Secretaries are usually always going round the world seeing things. If you go to New Zealand—I have been to New Zealand—when you get off the aeroplane, you are immediately confronted by dogs sniffing for food. Is that a good idea?

Sir Brian Bender: Yes, in the appropriate circumstances. As the Department said in the Treasury Minute that responded to your Report from the 2002 hearing, you cannot compare the situation in the UK with the situation in New Zealand because of the larger number of passengers and, indeed, the fact that we have to abide by EU regulations. Subject to that, having sniffer dogs is a good thing and Customs will have, or are moving up to, about 10 by this April.

Q180 Mr Steinberg: Ten? For the whole of the country?

Sir Brian Bender: Yes. They also have 3,500 detection officers who are trained in the detection and seizure of products of animal origin.

Q181 Mr Steinberg: Can I tell you of an experience that I had last year at Newcastle Airport. I was standing waiting for my bags to come off the carousel after coming back off holiday and, as usual, I just watched everybody's bags going round and round and my bag was not on the carousel going round and round. There was this one bag at the end going round and round, mine was not there. I was standing there like a big pudding and then suddenly I looked at the carousel and there was blood all over the place. I called the Customs Officer who came over and opened the bag and found a dead goat in the bag which was bleeding, the blood was all over the place. The bloke whose bag it was—I assume it was a bloke—whoever's bag it was had scarpered. That was illegal meat being brought into the country presumably.

Sir Brian Bender: I would assume so. Customs had made some 15,800 seizures in the year ending last March of illegal imports of this sort.

Q182 Mr Steinberg: The point I am trying to make is if it had not been for the fact that my bag had been lost and I was standing watching this bag going round—It was a good job it was a dead goat because it could have been somebody in the bag really, could it not? There was not a dog in sight. I have got off a plane from the Canary Islands and there were dogs sniffing you as you came in in case you were bringing in drugs. I would have thought a little dog at Newcastle Airport would stop this happening. I was told that this is a regular occurrence, people bringing in dead animals to eat presumably.

Sir Brian Bender: There is a large importation of meat products for personal consumption and a lot of that is illegal and that is why we have passed it over to Customs who have the expertise on dealing with illegal imports. As I said, the number of seizures was about 15,800 in the year to March 2004. They have increased their enforcement activity. That accounts for about 186 tonnes.

Chairman: On our draft programme for 21 May, Mr Steinberg, there is a hearing on illegal meat imports, so we very much hope that you are still a Member of the Committee on 21 May.

DEFRA and NFU

Q183 Mr Steinberg: I very much doubt it. I shall be consulting for DEFRA. I am finished, so if you ever need any consultants.

Sir Brian Bender: Judging by the representative of the National Farmers' Union who can sit in the back row and then make a contribution—

Mr Steinberg: I am very cheap. A pound of steak!

Q184 Mr Davidson: At paragraph 4.6 where it mentions North Yorkshire and Cumbria, 1,000 investigations into biosecurity offences, serious breaches in over 70, and that is only one part of the country, does that not make it apparent that farmers were behaving quite outrageously? Can I just clarify how many prosecutions took place there and what the penalties were?

Sir Brian Bender: I am in no better a position than on the previous question. We will provide a note.[18]

Q185 Mr Davidson: Can you give us the names of those who were involved rather than just the figures. I want to come back to this general question of what can be described as antisocial behaviour by farmers. I was depressed when I read paragraphs 4.6 and 4.7 that you seem to have an unwillingness to have proposals to link biosecurity and compensation. I know that one of the arguments is that farmers would be disputatious and would take you into court and there would be legal challenges. I have antisocial tenants in my constituency and the prospect of legal action has deterred councils from taken action in the past but ultimately we have had to do it. When there is antisocial behaviour by farmers and you feel that they might take you to court, why should you back off from that in circumstances where clearly the results of that antisocial behaviour could involve the taxpayer having to spend literally billions of pounds? Why is the Department so spineless?

Sir Brian Bender: There are two aspects. Looking backwards, the Department did introduce this in the Animal Health Bill and withdrew it because of the opposition in Parliament in order to get the rest of the legislation through. The question is what are we going to do?

Q186 Mr Davidson: That was the Lords, presumably?

Sir Brian Bender: It probably was the Lords.

Q187 Mr Davidson: Where there are lots of people who own farms and there are farmers in the Lords.

Sir Brian Bender: The Government, therefore, wished to introduce this power and in the end, in order to get the rest of the legislation through, withdrew that element. That is looking backwards. Looking forwards, as I say, we are considering good biosecurity with reduced charging, or the reverse, as part of cost sharing or part of our plans.

Q188 Mr Davidson: It is mentioned in the Report that Germany, Australia and the United States can withhold compensation and so on. Have you looked at what they have done and how they have done it and are there lessons there that you think we can learn?

Sir Brian Bender: There are lessons we can learn but also it says in this paragraph that the Dutch began doing it but discontinued the policy. We are looking internationally as well as at what we think we can do in this country.

Q189 Mr Davidson: Why did the Dutch discontinue it? It was because farmers were disputatious, is that correct?

Sir Brian Bender: I think they felt it was difficult to enforce.

Q190 Mr Davidson: It is the antisocial neighbours' issue, is it not?

Sir Brian Bender: It may not be as simple as disputatious; it may be that one cannot obtain reliable evidence in order to pursue it.

Q191 Mr Davidson: That is exactly the same problem that we have with antisocial tenants, issues of proof and so on. If you make a big enough effort and you do have the equivalent evictions it becomes a valuable learning experience for the rest. I see in the final sentence of 4.7 that farmers who deliberately and seriously breach rules will continue to be at the risk of prosecution. Can you clarify how many prosecutions there have been for these offences since 2001?

Sir Brian Bender: I will cover that in the same note.[19] I am sorry, but on this series of questions you have asked me, I have not come prepared. I apologise.

Q192 Mr Davidson: Could you give us the names as well. The final point I want to make is we are always told how hard up farmers are. Can you just clarify for us following Foot and Mouth how many farmers pulled out of agriculture and how many farms are now lying fallow?

Sir Brian Bender: The last time I appeared before this Committee we touched on some of that in the Report *Helping Farmers Adapt* and I did provide some material afterwards on some of these impacts. I will cover that in an updated version in a note.[20]

Q193 Mr Davidson: Can you give me an impression though? We are constantly told how difficult farming is.

Sir Brian Bender: There are fewer farmers than there were. The number of people employed in farming has gradually fallen over the years.

Q194 Mr Davidson: That is modernisation.

Sir Brian Bender: Some of that is to do with the restructuring that is going on in the industry.

Q195 Mr Davidson: People were getting huge amounts of money and it was an ideal opportunity for those who wanted to leave to do so. I wonder if you can just give me a feel of how many left.

[18] Ev 24

[19] Ev 23
[20] Ev 24

Sir Brian Bender: I do not think many did. What tended to happen was that restocking was at a less dense level, but I do not think many pulled out of the industry altogether.

Q196 Mr Davidson: Things were not as bad as they were making out then, were they?
Sir Brian Bender: Or the financial incentive to get out, as you were putting it, was not sufficiently high and they wished to carry on farming.
Mr Davidson: Thank you very much.

Q197 Chairman: Sir Brian, ladies, thank you very much for what has been a very interesting and lively and important hearing. Several times you have reminded us that we do look at this with the benefit of hindsight but I do not think you need to have the

benefit of hindsight to know that there were woeful inadequacies in the project management dealing with what admittedly was a grave crisis and there were deficiencies in the way you handled the evaluation and agreed compensation, so I am afraid you can expect a fairly robust Report from us, Sir Brian.
Sir Brian Bender: Can I just say one word, Chairman, which is the Government accepted in its response to the Independent Inquiry in writing that mistakes were made and the question, which I hope the Committee will also look at, is whether you believe not simply looking backwards but looking forwards that we are, as is the title of this Report, applying the lessons or not.
Chairman: We will try and be constructive and forward looking, Sir Brian. Thank you very much.

Supplementary memorandum submitted by the Department for Environment, Food and Rural Affairs

Questions 25-29 and 145,146,150,152 (Mrs Angela Browning):

BURNSIDE FARM, JIM DRING AND SWILL-FEEDING

Legislative controls

Article 21(2) of the Animal By-Products Order 1999 made it an offence to bring unprocessed catering waste onto any premises where ruminant animals, pigs or poultry were kept. Pigs were kept on the premises at Burnside Farm. Article 21(1)(c) required any person collecting or transporting unprocessed catering waste intended for feeding to pigs or poultry to take it without undue delay to an approved processing premises. It would therefore have been an offence under both provisions for Mr Waugh to store unprocessed catering waste at Burnside Farm. It was also an offence under Article 19 to feed unprocessed catering waste to ruminant animals, pigs and poultry or to allow such animals to have access to that material.

Inspection regime

Instructions to the State Veterinary Service were that operators who *processed* catering waste into swill were to be inspected four times a year. Operators who did not process catering waste, but who collected fully processed catering waste (swill) for *feeding* to their pigs, were only required to be inspected twice a year. The greater frequency of inspections to processors reflects the greater risk posed by unprocessed catering waste; processing was required to remove that risk.

Mr R Waugh was approved to feed processed catering waste to pigs at Burnside Farm. He was *not* approved to process catering waste into swill at Burnside Farm. Instead, he collected catering waste for processing at a separate premises. After processing, the resulting swill was then transported to Burnside Farm for feeding to Mr Waugh's pigs.

What did the SVS allow Mr Waugh to do?

Mr Waugh was approved under the Animal By-Products Order 1999 to feed swill (fully processed catering waste) at Burnside Farm and his operation was inspected by the State Veterinary Service twice a year for those purposes. The SVS did *not* allow Mr Waugh to feed unprocessed catering waste to his pigs (other than on one occasion, after FMD had been identified on the farm—see below). Neither did the SVS permit unprocessed catering waste to be *stored* on the farm.

However, some unprocessed catering waste was held *temporarily* in barrels on a hard standing in front of Burnside Farm, before being moved for processing at the processing premises. Judgement by District Judge James Prowse on 30 May 2002 in the case of Northumberland County Council v Robert Waugh concluded that whether or not it was taken direct to the processing premises or unloaded at Burnside Farm depended on which collector had collected it; one had fallen out with the processor and was told not to deliver to the processing premises. He therefore unloaded the material at Burnside Farm and it was taken to the processing premises shortly afterwards.

As Glenys Stacey explained, the SVS did not consider that unloading the catering waste on to a hard standing at the front of the farm was in breach of the Order. The hard standing adjoined the main road and was well away from the pigs or any activity involving the pigs. It was also understood that it was being taken to the processing premises without undue delay, as required by the Order.

Angela Browning referred to a map of the farm (which we have not seen) and commented that the area where the unprocessed catering waste was held temporarily was in close proximity to the pig sheds numbered 4 and 5. However, the position of the hard standing and the layout of the pig operation were such that there was not considered to be any possibility of the pigs having access to the unprocessed catering waste. The unprocessed catering waste was held temporarily on the hard standing adjacent to the road. A low wall separated the hard standing from the pig sheds. Also on the hard standing, adjacent to the wall, was an enclosed tank into which processed swill was piped from a reception tank located between the wall and the back of pig shed 4. Pedestrian entry to the pig operation was through a gate at the far end of the hard standing with vehicle entry a further 20 yards down, on the far side of the slurry tank. Pigs were unloaded or loaded at a loading dock adjacent to pig shed number 1. From there the pigs were routed via a walled path into all sheds. Pigs entering or leaving sheds 4 and 5 thus did so via the end of the shed furthest away from the hard standing.

Unprocessed catering waste was found at Burnside Farm when FMD was identified there. Before then, the SVS had never been aware of any unprocessed catering waste being stored there, although fully processed swill was stored. Jim Dring's personal statement confirms this view, but speculates, with the benefit of hindsight, that unprocessed catering waste must nevertheless have been fed to the pigs at Burnside Farm in addition to the fully processed swill.

Did Mr Dring fulfil his regulatory duties?

The instructions to the SVS advised staff that during their six-monthly visits to those receiving fully processed swill they should remind the recipient that swill-fed pigs were only to be moved direct to a slaughterhouse. SVS staff were also to check that the swill was being handled properly and presented no disease risk and that the conditions of the authority to transport the swill were being complied with. Mr Dring carried out his visits in accordance with those instructions and his assessment of the situation at the time. He examined the pigs for signs of disease and ensured that Mr Waugh was aware of his responsibilities associated with swill feeding. He took action when welfare problems were identified and checked that the necessary remedial action was carried out.

Management supervision

The Divisional Veterinary Manager of each Animal Health Divisional Office is responsible for ensuring that inspection visits are carried out at the required times and in accordance with the instructions, as was the case with the visits to Burnside Farm.

Did the SVS allow unprocessed catering waste to be fed to pigs at Burnside Farm?

The SVS allowed unprocessed catering waste to be fed to pigs at Burnside Farm on only one occasion. That was after FMD had been confirmed in the herd and while slaughter of the herd was awaited. The pigs needed to be fed, pending epidemiological investigation, sampling and ultimate slaughter. There was no processed swill on site and in the circumstances of the restrictions on the farm, it was decided to allow the feeding of unprocessed catering waste which was present in the bins on Mr Waugh's lorry.

Is the SVS or Mr Waugh responsible for the outbreak of FMD?

Individuals are responsible for their own compliance with the legislation. Where they do not comply, they can expect to face the consequences when the non-compliance is detected. Potential sanctions include the removal of their approval to operate, and prosecution. In this case, it was Mr Waugh who fed unprocessed catering waste to his pigs and it was Mr Waugh who was successfully prosecuted for that breach of the Animal By-Products Order 1999. Although enforcement bodies can monitor and check compliance with the law and discourage and seek to identify breaches, they do not maintain a constant presence at every operation; nor should they. They adopt a risk-based approach to enforcement, as was the case with the controls on swill processors and feeders (explained above).

Questions 41 and 159 (Mr David Curry):

We should clarify what was said during the hearing about vaccinating different species during an outbreak. It is true that we are currently envisaging vaccination being the most likely for cattle, but it is not ruled out for other species. Our current thoughts are set out in the vaccination scenarios on our website: http://defraweb/animalh/diseases/fmd/pdf/vaccinationscenarios.pdf

However, as noted during the hearing, the cost benefit analysis currently in train will further inform our thinking in this area.

Questions 52 and 176 (Mr Gerry Steinberg and Mr Brian Jenkins):

Q. *Are Valuers from 2001 on the current list of valuers and are any of the valuation firms we were/are in dispute with on the current list?*

A. Since 2001, the Department has compiled a list of over 300 Approved Valuers for use in a future animal health disease outbreak. This list includes some of the individuals who carried out Foot and Mouth Disease (FMD) valuations during 2001.

The Department neither has, nor has been given, evidence that would allow it to pursue legal actions in either a civil or criminal context against valuers, individuals or firms, engaged in 2001. The Department is currently in commercial dispute with a number of valuer firms in relation to the fees charged for valuations undertaken during the 2001 FMD outbreak. I should emphasise that we are not in dispute over the professional competency of these firms, or the individual valuers in undertaking such valuations. Our concerns arise solely from the basis of the valuer's fees chargeable for valuations undertaken in 2001.

One of the lessons we learned as a result of the 2001 FMD outbreak is that we will only deal with valuers who meet our eligibility requirements, have the appropriate economic and financial standing, and who can deliver the requisite services at reasonable economic cost to agreed contractual arrangements. The fact that the Department is in commercial dispute still with some of these valuer firms is not in itself sufficient or adequate reason to exclude, some or all, of the valuers on the approved list that work for those firms.

It is vital that we have a sufficient pool of qualified and experienced valuers across the country to turn to in any future outbreak. It is essential that the process of valuation allows rapid slaughter because rapid slaughter reduces the overall costs of disease eradication.

Subject to the criteria above, the Department would consider requests from valuers to be added to our list, and so be able to value livestock in future outbreaks. Improvements in procedures and documentation control give us confidence that the potential for excessive valuations in the future would be hugely restricted in comparison to 2001 though it must be recognised that valuations in the midst of an unprecedented animal health disease outbreak, and without market demand and supply information is challenging.

Questions 53-55 (Mr Gerry Steinberg):

We are currently in discussion with nine valuer firms regarding disputed fee charges (sums in dispute are £617K). In addition a further 20 valuers claimed £203K over and above their entitlement in 2001, but these claims have not been pursued. Forensic analysis has highlighted that overpayments have occurred, and in the absence of evidence that they are justified, the Department will seek to recover the overpayments made. We have recently settled the largest single dispute, and have made offers to settle others where appropriate.

We cannot issue a list of names of those involved with the outstanding cases, because this may prejudice any future or current civil proceedings. Settlements already agreed are the subject of confidentiality agreements.

Questions 76, 77, 82, 83, 84, 86, 87,88, 89, 90, 91, 92 (Mr Brian Jenkins and Mr Ian Davidson):

Paragraph 2.10 of the NAO Report

There is no formal target for reducing the number of breaches of the livestock movement restrictions. The breaches found in the traffic exercise reported in paragraph 2.10 of the NAO Report were wide ranging, and included offences relating to animal welfare as well as to the livestock movement rules themselves. Many of the breaches were minor. For example transposition of two digits within a holding number on a movement document counts as a breach, but can be put right very easily.

All non-compliances found during the exercise (23% of the 383 vehicles engaged in animal transport) were dealt with either by way of advice or verbal or written warnings. No prosecutions were taken.

There have been no further national exercises since. We will be consulting with the Association of Chief Police Officers with a view to holding regular national exercises in future.

Paragraph 2.9 of the NAO Report

All Local Authorities in England and Wales undertaking animal health and welfare enforcement activities are signed up to the Framework Agreement on delivery of services in Animal Health and Welfare through their representative body LACORS (Local Authority Coordinators of Regulatory Services). This has been developed to include regular liaison and consultation between Local Authorities and the State Veterinary Service, agreeing annual Local Authority service delivery plans, based upon a joint risk assessment process.

It is supported by a web based secure enforcement database—the Animal Health & Welfare Management & Enforcement System—which allows Local Authorities to record enforcement activities, results and actions. This information is accessible to all Local Authorities and the State Veterinary Service. For the period January to December 2003, 71 Local Authorities were entering data on this system. These Local Authorities cover the areas that represent a significant percentage of known livestock movements. This data indicates that 191 prosecutions were initiated; of these 58 convictions were achieved, nine cases have been withdrawn and two are subject to appeal. We do not have information available on the remaining cases, as we do not receive detailed information on prosecutions; the prosecuting Local Authority holds specific information regarding the outcomes of cases, including the level of fines imposed by the court.

An annual report is submitted to Parliament on the number of prosecutions initiated by Local Authorities under the Animal Health Act.

Successful prosecutions and the level of penalty (paragraph 2.9)

This information is not currently collected centrally; however, in some cases, Local Authorities have shared this information with us (see Q184 below).

In addition to the Local Authorities, Defra also prosecute for Cattle Identification offences discovered by the British Cattle Movement Service/Rural Payments Agency. From 2001 to date, 25 such prosecutions have taken place; of these two offenders were imprisoned, two were given suspended sentences, six were given conditional discharges and the remainder were fined.

The two offenders who were imprisoned for breaches of Cattle Identification Regulations were Kelvin Smith (11 weeks in 2003) and Haydn Roberts (four weeks in 2004).

Fines for the breaches of Cattle Identification Regulations mentioned above total £26,645.

We have taken steps to inform magistrates about these offences. We would hope that the punishments would be commensurate with the crime committed and that they would prove to be a deterrent.

Paragraph 4.6

In North Yorkshire, prosecutions were taken in 12 cases, sometimes for multiple offences. Fines ranged from £50 for each offence to £300.

In Cumbria, prosecutions were taken in three cases, one of which resulted in a fine of £300 and the other two 12 months Conditional Discharges.

We do not hold detailed information on prosecutions; the prosecuting Local Authority holds specific information regarding the cases.

However, the relevant Local Authorities have provided the following details:

Date of Hearing	Defendant	Result
13/9/01	Ronald George Mark	£300 fine
2/10/01	John Kenneth Poole	£200 fine + £55 costs
2/10/01	John McIntrye	£300 fine + £55 costs
8/10/01	Tracey Michelle Fawcett	£200 fine + £145 costs (2 offences)
10/10/01	Derek Taylor	£100 fine +£100 costs
12/10/01	Patrick Wharmby	£100 fine +£62 costs
12/10/01	Kathleen Smith	£100 fine +£62 costs
26/10/01	Leslie Moore	£100 fine + £63.42 costs (2 offences)
5/11/01	Stephen Ridle	12 month conditional discharge
15/11/01	Robert Heliwell	£300 fine + £90 costs (2 offences)
16/11/01	Kenneth Harold Harrison	£100 fine + £130 costs
22/11/01	Robert David Howard	£250 fine + £171.76 costs
3/12/01	Stephen Hill	£225 fine + £175 costs (2 offences)
3/12/01	John Tevaski	12 month conditional discharge
3/5/02	Peter G Hutchinson	£250 + £50 costs

Prosecutions within controlled zones there have been for these offences since 2001

Controlled zones around infected premises only apply during a disease outbreak. There have been no outbreaks since 2001 and there have therefore been no offences. In the event of an outbreak, biosecurity rules would be rigorously enforced because of the important role that good biosecurity has been shown to play in preventing the spread of disease.

Our database records checks on biosecurity (cleansing and disinfection) on farms, at markets and in livestock vehicles. During 2003 and 2004, some non-compliances were recorded for farm premises but there were no prosecutions.

Question 115 (Mr Ian Davidson):

Defra inadvertently made a payment of £240,715 for animals valued but in the event were not slaughtered. The farmer received three valuations, only two should have been paid. Unfortunately due to the size and scale of the exercise all three were sent for payment. The erroneous payment was recovered in full and the line was withdrawn from the EU claim. There was no evidence of fraud.

Question 132 (Chairman):

I understand that the NFU have also written to you to confirm the views I expressed at the hearing that the NFU accept the principle of vaccination. They have made it clear that if the UK was faced with another FMD outbreak, then all appropriate options to control the outbreak should be considered and this very clearly includes the potential use of vaccination as part of the overall control strategy.

Questions 137-138 (Mr Gerry Steinberg):

The Cost Benefit Analysis covers the costs and impacts of outbreaks of FMD (and the subsequent response) in England, Scotland and Wales and examines four broad control options:

(a) Culling of infected premises and epidemiologically linked holdings (dangerous contacts).

(b) Strategy (a) plus contiguous cull.

(c) Strategy (a) plus vaccination to live of cattle only.

(d) Strategy (a) plus vaccination to live of cattle and sheep.

This will enable us to make informed policy decisions on disease control strategies in any future outbreak. This information was not available in 2001. The report will be published next month, and we shall be making the full report publicly available via our website.

Question 192 (Mr Ian Davidson):

Following the FMD outbreak in 2001, ADAS was commissioned to conduct a telephone survey of approximately 1,000 farmers. The aim was to establish how they had been affected by the outbreak and their future intentions.

The study found that by February 2002, 78% of infected premises and 65% of premises classified as Dangerous Contacts intended to restock and continue farming as soon as possible. Only 6% of those classified as a foot and mouth infected premise indicated that they would definitely be "moving out of farming". 25% indicated that they would "definitely" or "possibly" move some or all of the land on their holding into environmental schemes.

Farming trends have been monitored using the agricultural census data. The total number of agricultural holdings in England with cattle, sheep or pigs has fallen by less than 1% since 2001 and the livestock market has remained buoyant throughout this period.

Sir Brian Bender KCB
Permanent Secretary

17 March 2005

Supplementary memorandum submitted by the National Farmers' Union

At the hearing on 23 February from Defra witnesses on the NAO's Report, "Foot and mouth disease: Applying the Lessons" on 23 February, the issue was raised of the current position of farmers concerning the use of vaccination as part of a control strategy for any future outbreak of foot and mouth disease (questions 120–134 of the transcript of uncorrected evidence refer). The NFU representative present at the hearing indicated that the NFU would write to you to confirm our views on this matter.

The NFU welcomes the opportunity to set out our position on the principle of the use of vaccination as a control strategy during an outbreak of foot and mouth disease (FMD).

There has been some misunderstanding about the NFU's position on the issue of vaccination during the 2001 FMD outbreak. The NFU has never been opposed to the principle of the use of vaccination to control an FMD outbreak. However, during the 2001 FMD epidemic the use of vaccination was only ever authorised by the European Commission for limited use in Cumbria and Devon. At the stage that this authorisation was granted there were clear signs that the disease was close to being under control in Devon, and that we were quickly getting to that position in Cumbria. In addition there was no compelling epidemiological and veterinary opinion at the time saying that the use of vaccination was an appropriate measure. This coupled with the complicated issues of the status of products from animals that had been vaccinated and the views of the major players in the meat and milk supply chains, led the NFU to the position of not supporting the use of vaccination as a control strategy in those two instances.

Since the 2001 FMD outbreak the issue of the use of vaccination as an FMD control strategy has moved on considerably. Notably there is a new EU FMD directive which clearly sets out that the use of emergency vaccination must be considered from the start of any future FMD outbreak where measures in addition to the culling of infected animals and dangerous contacts are needed. This new directive also clearly sets out the process for dealing with products from animals that have been vaccinated, and whilst these measures would clearly have an impact on the livestock industry at least the position is more certain than in 2001, and there is now no requirement for the marking of products from animals that have been treated at the point of sale. Although there is no public health issue with these products, nevertheless the NFU strongly believes that should we find ourselves in the position in the UK of needing to vaccinate animals we would need a repetition of the very clear and unambiguous messages which the Food Standards Agency has already given, and a clear communication message across the food industry.

Other changes on the issue of vaccination include developments on the testing process used to distinguish between infected and vaccinated animals. The testing process known as the NSP test (Non Structural Protein test) has been evaluated and validated in some detail and we understand that this test would be able to be used effectively to prove freedom from infection where vaccination has been used. There is also now a wider selection of vaccines to deal with the various strains of virus and these vaccines should now be available very quickly during the early stages of an FMD outbreak.

As a result of these developments the NFU is much more content on the efficacy of the vaccination process, and on the supply chain issues than we were. There are still issues surrounding the impact of restrictions on exporting products from animals that have been vaccinated, despite the fact the during the discussions on the EU FMD directive the length of the restrictions were reduced from 12 months after the last vaccination to six months. This issue would need to form part of the deliberations on deciding the most appropriate control strategy.

This leads us to the important issue of the process of deciding on the most effective control strategy during an FMD outbreak. Defra have produced a decision tree as part of their contingency plan and we very much support this approach. Defra have also commissioned a Cost Benefit Analysis (CBA) study of various FMD Control Strategies. This is a vital piece of work which will greatly enhance the understanding of the effectiveness and impact of various disease control strategies and we look forward to seeing the final results.

The NFU is fully committed to working with Defra on the contingency plan, including participating in national and local exercises so that we maintain a state of readiness for an FMD outbreak. We are also keen to further develop thinking on control strategies for FMD and other diseases once the CBA has been completed.

The NFU never wants to see a repeat of the 2001 FMD outbreak. Our overriding concern is the welfare of our animals and we believe that everything possible should be done to prevent the FMD virus entering the country. This is an integral part of Government's obligations under the Animal Health and Welfare Strategy. However, if the UK was faced with another FMD outbreak, all appropriate options to control the outbreak should be considered and this very clearly includes the potential use of vaccination as part of the overall control strategy.

As the leading representative body of some 55,000 farmers in England and Wales the NFU would want to be sure that the recommended control strategy is based on sound veterinary and epidemiological advice, and that the wider ramifications of the strategy including the impact on meat and milk supply chains and the longer term impact on the livestock sector have been fully considered. The overriding objective must be to devise and follow a strategy that controls the outbreak, limits the number of animals that have to be slaughtered, and limits the impact that the outbreak would have on the country, particularly the livestock sector and the wider rural economy.

Meurig Raymond, MBE, FRAgS
Vice President

9 March 2005

Map of Burnside Farm submitted by the Department for Environment, Food and Rural Affairs

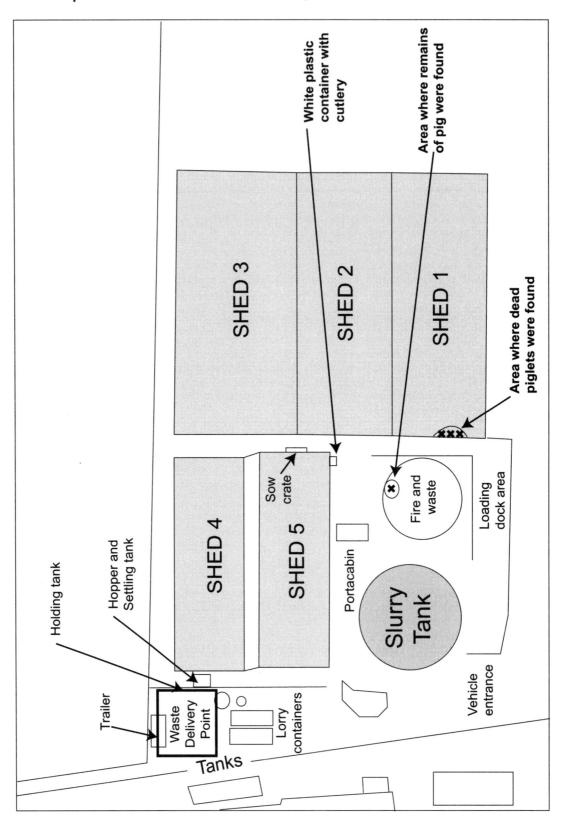

Printed in the United Kingdom by The Stationery Office Limited
11/2005   311020   19585

ISBN 0-215-02603-9

9 780215 026033